BOOKS BY DR. JOHN C. MAXWELL CAN TEACH YOU HOW TO BE A REAL SUCCESS

RELATIONSHIPS

Be a People Person
Becoming a Person of Influence
The Power of Influence
The Power of Partnership
in the Church
Relationships 101
The Treasure of a Friend
Winning with People
25 Ways to Win with People

EQUIPPING

Developing the Leaders
Around You
Equipping 101
Partners in Prayer
Your Road Map for Success
Your Road Map for
Success Workbook
Success One Day at a Time
The 17 Indisputable
Laws of Teamwork
The 17 Essential Qualities
of a Team Player

ATTITUDE

Be All You Can Be
Failing Forward
The Power of Thinking
Living at the Next Level
Think on These Things
The Winning Attitude
Your Bridge to a Better Future
The Power of Attitude

LEADERSHIP

The Leader's Greatest Return
Leadershift
How to Lead When Your
Boss Can't (or Won't)
The 21 Indispensable
Qualities of a Leader
The 21 Irrefutable
Laws of Leadership
The 21 Most Powerful
Minutes in a Leader's Day
Developing the Leader
Within You Workbook
Developing the Leader
Within You 2.0
The Power of Leadership
The Right to Lead

SUCCESS IS
A CHOICE

SUCCESS
IS A
CHOICE

MAKE THE CHOICES THAT
MAKE YOU SUCCESSFUL

JOHN C. MAXWELL

**HARPERCOLLINS
LEADERSHIP**

AN IMPRINT OF HARPERCOLLINS

John C. Maxwell
PUBLISHING

Success Is a Choice

© 2020 John C. Maxwell

Published by HarperCollins Leadership, an imprint of HarperCollins Focus LLC.

Success Is a Choice is adapted from material previously published in *Beyond Talent*.

Published in association with Yates &Yates, www.yates2.com

Any internet addresses, phone numbers, or company or product information printed in this book are offered as a resource and are not intended in any way to be or to imply an endorsement by HarperCollins Leadership, nor does HarperCollins Leadership vouch for the existence, content, or services of these sites, phone numbers, companies, or products beyond the life of this book.

ISBN 978-0-7852-3859-1 (HC)
ISBN 978-0-7852-3860-7 (eBook)

Printed in the United States of America
23 24 25 26 27 LBC 7 6 5 4 3

CONTENTS

ACKNOWLEDGMENTS

I want to say thank you to Charlie Wetzel and the rest of the team who assisted me with the formation and publication of this book. And to the people in my organizations who support it. You all add incredible value to me, which allows me to add value to others. Together, we're making a difference!

CHAPTER 1

COMMIT TO CHOICES
THAT BRING SUCCESS

Where does success come from? French poet and dramatist Edouard Pailleron pointed out, "Have success and there will always be fools to say that you have talent." When people achieve great things, others often explain their accomplishments by simply attributing everything to talent. But that is a false and misleading way of looking at success. If talent alone were enough, then why would you and I know highly talented people who are not highly successful?

Talent is never enough. Peter Drucker, the father of modern management, said, "There seems to be little correlation between a man's effectiveness and his intelligence, his imagination, or his knowledge . . . Intelligence, imagination, and knowledge are essential resources, but only effectiveness converts them into results. By themselves, they only set limits to what can be contained."[1] If talent were enough, then the most effective and influential people would always be the most talented ones. But that is often not the case. Consider this:

- More than fifty percent of all CEOs of *Fortune* 500 companies had C or C- averages in college.
- Sixty-five percent of all U.S. senators came from the bottom half of their school classes.
- Seventy-five percent of U.S. presidents were in the Lower-Half Club in school.
- More than fifty percent of millionaire entrepreneurs never finished college![2]

Clearly talent isn't everything. So what makes the difference?

DO YOU HAVE WHAT IT TAKES?

So what does it take to succeed? Can anyone be successful? And where does talent fit in at all? Here's what I believe:

1. Everyone Has Talent

People have equal value, but not equal giftedness. Some people seem to be blessed with a multitude of talents. Most of us have fewer abilities. But know this: all of us have something we can do well.

In their book *Now, Discover Your Strengths*, Marcus Buckingham and Donald O. Clifton state that every person is capable of doing something better than the next ten thousand people. And they support that assertion with solid research. They call this area the strength zone, and they encourage everyone to find it and make the most of it. It doesn't matter how aware you are of your abilities, how you feel about yourself, or whether you previously have achieved success. You are who you are, and you do have talent, which you can develop.

2. Develop the Talent You Have, Not the One You Want

If I asked you who would be more successful, the person who relies on his talent alone or the person who realizes his talent and develops it, the answer would be obvious. Then I'll ask you this question: Why do most people spend the majority of their time focused on strengthening their weaknesses?

One thing I teach people at my conferences is to stop working on their weaknesses and start working on their strengths. (By this I mean abilities, not attitude or character issues, which *must* be addressed.) It has been my observation that people can increase their ability in an area by only two points on a scale of 1 to 10. For example, if your natural talent in an area is a 4, with hard work you may rise to a 6. In other words, you can go from a little below average to a little above average. But let's say you find a place where you are a 7; you have the potential to become a 9, maybe even a 10, if it's your greatest area of strength and you work exceptionally hard! That helps you advance from 1 in 10,000 talent to 1 in 100,000 talent—but only if you do the other things needed to maximize your talent.

3. Anyone Can Make Choices That Will Add Value to Talent

So if you should focus on developing your best talent, and not your weaknesses, where should you expend your energy? On your choices. *The key choices you make—apart from the natural talent you already have—will set you apart from others who have talent alone.* Orator, attorney, and political leader William Jennings Bryan said, "Destiny is not a matter of chance, it is a matter of choice; it is not a thing to be waited for, it is a thing to be achieved."

Success is your choice. If you're willing to commit yourself to making the right choices, you can achieve success. I've discovered fourteen key choices that can make a difference.

- Commit to Choices That Bring Success
- Believe in Yourself
- Fire Up Your Passion
- Initiate Action
- Focus Your Energy
- Value Preparation
- Embrace Practice
- Embody Perseverance
- Demonstrate Courage
- Become More Teachable
- Develop Strong Character
- Cultivate Good Relationships
- Commit to Responsibility
- Lean In to Teamwork

Make these choices, and you can become the successful person you've always desired to be.

YOU CAN DO IT!

I believe the ideas in this book can help you. Life is a matter of choices, and every choice you make makes you. What will you do for your career? Whom will you marry? Where will you live? How much education will you get? What will you do with today? But one of the most important choices you will make is *who will you become*! Life is not merely a matter of holding and playing a good hand as you would hope to do in a card game. What you start with isn't up to you. *Talent* is God-given. Life is doing a great job of playing the hand you have been dealt. That is determined by your choices.

WHO YOU ARE + *RIGHT CHOICES* = SUCCESS

If you're willing to commit to making the right choices, you can reach your potential and fulfill your destiny.

I was reading a book by Dr. Seuss to my grandchildren called *Oh, the Places You'll Go!* In it, I found a wonderful truth. It said,

> You have brains in your head.
> You have feet in your shoes.
> You can steer yourself
> Any direction you choose.[3]

I believe that with all my heart. My prayer is that this book will help you steer yourself in the right direction and make right choices that will empower you to become a success.

Chapter 2

Believe in Yourself

The first and greatest obstacle to success for most people is their belief in themselves. Once people figure out where their sweet spot is (the area where they are most gifted), what often hinders them isn't lack of talent. It's lack of trust in themselves, which is a self-imposed limitation. Lack of belief can act as a ceiling on potential. However, when people believe in themselves, they unleash power in themselves and resources around them that almost immediately take them to a higher level. Your potential is a picture of what you can become. Belief helps you see the picture and reach for it.

BELIEFS WORTH BUYING INTO

I don't know what your talent is, but I do know this: it will not be lifted to its highest level unless you also have belief. If you want to become your best, you need to believe your best. You need to . . .

1. BELIEVE IN YOUR POTENTIAL

Your potential is a picture of what you can become. Inventor Thomas Edison remarked, "If we did all the things we are capable of doing, we would literally astonish ourselves."

Indian statesman Mohandas Gandhi said, "The difference between what we do and what we are capable of doing would suffice to solve most of the world's problems." Closer to home, it would also suffice to solve most of our *individual* problems. We must first believe in our potential if we are to do what we're capable of.

Too many people fall far short of their real potential. John Powell, author of *The Secret of Staying in Love,* estimates that the average person reaches only ten percent of his potential, sees only ten percent of the beauty that is all around him, hears only ten percent of its music and poetry, smells only ten percent of its fragrance, and tastes only ten percent of the deliciousness of being alive. Most neither see nor seize their potential.

Executive coach Joel Garfinkle recounts a story by writer Mark Twain in which a man died and met Saint Peter at the pearly gates. Immediately realizing that Saint Peter was a wise and knowledgeable individual, the man inquired, "Saint Peter, I have been interested in military history for many years. Tell me, who was the greatest general of all time?"

Saint Peter quickly responded, "Oh, that's a simple question. It's that man right over there."

"You must be mistaken," responded the man, now very perplexed. "I knew that man on earth and he was just a common laborer."

"That's right, my friend," assured Saint Peter. "He would

have been the greatest general of all time, if he had been a general."[1]

Cartoonist Charles Schulz offered this comparison: "Life is a ten-speed bike. Most of us have gears we never use." What are we saving those gears for? It's not good to travel through life without breaking a sweat. So what's the problem? Most of the time it's self-imposed limitations. They limit us as much as real ones. Life is difficult enough as it is. We make it more difficult when we impose *additional* limitations on ourselves. Industrialist Charles Schwab observed, "When a man has put a limit on what he *will* do, he has put a limit on what he can do."

In *If It Ain't Broke . . . Break It!* Robert J. Kriegel and Louis Patler wrote,

> We don't have a clue as to what people's limits are. All the tests, stopwatches, and finish lines in the world can't measure human potential. When someone is pursuing their dream, they'll go far beyond what seems to be their limitations. The potential that exists within us is limitless and largely untapped . . . When you think of limits, you create them.[2]

We often put too much emphasis on mere physical challenges and obstacles, and give too little credence to psychological and emotional ones. Sharon Wood, the first North American woman to climb Mount Everest, learned some things about that after making her successful climb. She said, "I discovered it wasn't a matter of physical strength, but a matter of psychological strength. The conquest lay within my own mind to penetrate those barriers of self-imposed limitations and get through to that good stuff—the stuff called potential, ninety percent of which we rarely use."[3]

Several years ago I was invited to Mobile, Alabama, to speak to six hundred NFL coaches and scouts at the Senior Bowl. That's the game played by two teams of college seniors who have been invited to participate because they are believed to have NFL potential. In the morning I taught from *The 17 Indisputable Laws of Teamwork*, which had just been published. And in the afternoon I attended a workout session in which the players were tested for running speed, reaction time, jumping ability, and so forth.

One of the coaches in attendance, Dick Vermeil, chatted with me as I watched. At one point he said, "You know, we can measure many of their skills, but it's impossible to measure the heart. Only the player can determine that."

Your potential is really up to you. It doesn't matter what others might think. It doesn't matter where you came from. It doesn't even matter what you might have believed about yourself at a previous time in your life. It's about what lies within you and whether you can bring it out.

There's a story about a farm boy from Colorado who loved to hike and rock climb. One day while climbing in the mountains, he found an eagle's nest with an egg in it. He took the egg from the nest, and when he got home, he put it under a hen along with her other eggs.

Since the eagle hatched among chicks, he thought he was a chicken. He learned chicken behavior from his "mother" and scratched in the chicken yard along with his "siblings." He didn't know any better. And when he sometimes felt strange stirrings within him, he didn't know what to do with them, so he ignored them or suppressed them. After all, if he was a chicken, he should behave like a chicken.

Then one day an eagle flew over the farm, and the

chicken-yard eagle looked up and saw him. In that moment he realized he wanted to be like that eagle. He wanted to fly high. He wanted to go to the mountain peaks he saw in the distance. He spread his wings, which were much larger and stronger than those of his siblings. Suddenly he understood that he was like that eagle. Though he had never flown before, he possessed the instinct and the capabilities. He spread his wings once more, and he flew, unsteadily at first, but then with greater power and control. As he soared and climbed, he knew he had finally discovered his true self.

Phillips Brooks, writer of the song "O Little Town of Bethlehem," remarked, "When you discover you've been leading only half a life, the other half is going to haunt you until you develop it." Not only is that true, but I'd also say this: not reaching your potential is a real tragedy. To reach your potential, you must first believe in your potential, and determine to live way beyond average.

2. BELIEVE IN YOURSELF

It's one thing to believe that you possess remarkable potential. It's another thing to have enough faith in yourself that you think you can fulfill it. When it comes to believing in themselves, some people are agnostic! That's not only a shame; it also keeps them from becoming what they could be. Psychologist and philosopher William James emphasized that "there is but one cause of human failure. And that is man's lack of faith in his true self."

People who believe in themselves get better jobs and perform better in them than those who don't. Martin Seligman, professor of psychology at the University of Pennsylvania, did some research at a major life insurance company and found that the salespeople who expected to succeed sold thirty-seven percent more insurance than those who didn't.[4]

The impact of belief in self begins early. Some researchers assert that when it comes to academic achievement in school, there is a greater correlation between self-confidence and achievement than there is between IQ and achievement.

Attorney and marketing expert Kerry Randall observed, "Successful people believe in themselves, especially when others do not." That's no more evident than in sports. Coaches have told me that self-confidence within players is especially important in tight ball games. During crunch time, some players want the ball. Others want to hide. The ones who want the ball are the self-confident ones.

People with confidence live by a credo that is said to hang in the office of golfer Arnold Palmer. It reads,

> If you think you are beaten, you are.
> If you think you dare not, you don't.
> If you'd like to win, but think you can't
> It's almost certain you won't . . .
> Life's battles don't always go
> To the stronger or faster man,
> But soon or late, the man who wins
> Is the man who thinks he can.[5]

Only with belief in yourself will you be able to reach your potential.

3. BELIEVE IN YOUR MISSION

What else is necessary to lift a person's talent? Believing in what you are doing. In fact, even if the odds are against your accomplishing what you desire, confidence will help you. William James asserted, "The one thing that will guarantee the successful conclusion of a doubtful undertaking is faith in the beginning that you can do it." How does this kind of belief help?

Belief in your mission will empower you. Having confidence in what you are doing gives you the power to achieve it. Architect Frank Lloyd Wright noted, "The thing always happens that you really believe in; and the belief in a thing makes it happen." Confident people can usually evaluate a task before undertaking it and know whether they can do it. In that belief is great power.

Belief in your mission will encourage you. A woman with a will to win will have her naysayers. A man on a mission will have his critics. What often allows such people to keep going in a negative environment? Belief in the mission.

Playwright Neil Simon advised, "Don't listen to those who say, 'It's not done that way.' Maybe it's not, but maybe you'll do it anyway. Don't listen to those who say, 'You're taking too big a chance.' Michelangelo would have painted the Sistine floor, and it would surely be rubbed out today."[6] Simon knew this firsthand. He was awarded four Tony Awards, one Drama Desk Award, and the 1991 Pulitzer Prize for Drama.

Obviously he believed in what he did.

Belief in your mission will enlarge you. The more you believe in your potential, yourself, and your mission, the more you will be able to accomplish. If you keep believing, you will someday find yourself doing what you once considered impossible.

Actor Christopher Reeve had that perspective, and it carried him far. He once told an audience,

America has a tradition many nations probably envy: we frequently achieve the impossible. That's part of our national character. That's what got us from one coast to another. That's what got us the largest economy in the world. That's what got us to the moon. On the wall of my room when I was in rehab was a picture of the space shuttle blasting off, autographed by every astronaut now at NASA. On top of the picture says, "We found nothing is impossible." That should be our motto . . . It's something that we as a nation must do together. So many of our dreams at first seem impossible, then they seem improbable, and then, when we summon the will, they soon become inevitable. If we can conquer outer space, we should be able to conquer inner space, too. The frontier of the brain, the central nervous system, and all the afflictions of the body that destroy so many lives, and rob . . . so much potential.[7]

Do you believe in your mission? Are you confident that you can accomplish great tasks? Do you expect to achieve your goals? These are necessary ingredients to lift your talent from potential to fruition.

I need to say one more thing about mission. It needs to include people. Only a life lived for others is worthwhile. As you fulfill your mission, will others around you say . . .

"My life is *better* as a result," or

"My life is *worse* as a result"?

If you think it won't be the former, then the mission may not be worth doing.

One of my prized possessions is a simple crystal paperweight. It doesn't have an especially artistic design. It's not especially valuable monetarily. But it means a lot to me because of what is engraved in it and who gave it to me. It says,

John—
>   Pastor, Mentor, Friend
>   "Thank you for believing in me."
>   Love,
>   Dan

It was a gift from Dan Reiland, who worked with me for twenty years as a staff member, as my second in command, and then as a senior vice president at one of my companies. Dan is someone I would go to battle with. He's like a kid brother to me. The mission we pursued together made *both* of us better. That's the kind of person you want working with you—and the kind of result.

BELIEF IN ACTION

So how do you believe in yourself? You tap into a natural chain of actions that begins with belief and ends with positive action:

BELIEF DETERMINES EXPECTATIONS

If you want your talent to be lifted to its highest level, then you don't begin by focusing on your talent. You begin by harnessing the power of your mind. Your beliefs control everything you do. Accomplishment is more than a matter of working harder or smarter. It's also a matter of believing positively. Someone called it the "sure enough" syndrome. If you expect to fail, sure enough, you will. If you expect to succeed, sure enough, you will. You will become on the outside what you believe on the inside.

Personal breakthroughs begin with a change in your beliefs.

Why? Because your beliefs determine your expectations, and your expectations determine your actions. A belief is a habit of mind in which confidence becomes a conviction that we embrace. In the long run, a belief is more than an idea that a person possesses. It is an idea that possesses a person. Benjamin Franklin said, "Blessed is he who expects nothing, for he shall never be disappointed." If you want to achieve something in life, you have to be willing to be disappointed. You need to expect to succeed. Does that mean you always will? No. You will fail. You will make mistakes. But if you expect to win, you maximize your talent, and you keep trying. You will eventually succeed.

Attorney Kerry Randall said, "Contrary to popular opinion, life does not get better by chance, life gets better by change. And this change always takes place inside; it is the change of thought that creates the better life." Improvement comes from change, but change requires confidence. For that reason, you need to make confidence in yourself a priority. You need to put believing in your potential, yourself, your mission, and your fellow human beings at the top of your list. President Franklin Delano Roosevelt asserted, "The only limit to our realization of tomorrow will be our doubts of today." Don't let your doubts cause your expector to expire.

Harvey McKay tells the story of a professor who stood before a class of thirty senior molecular biology students. Before he passed out the final exam, he stated, "I have been privileged to be your instructor this semester, and I know how hard you have worked to prepare for this test. I also know most of you are off to medical school or grad school next fall. I am well aware of how much pressure you are under to keep your GPAs up, and because I am confident that you know this material, I am prepared to offer an automatic B to anyone who opts to skip taking the final exam."

The relief was audible. A number of students jumped up from their desks, thanking their professor for the lifeline he had thrown them.

"Any other takers?" he asked. "This is your last opportunity."

One more student decided to go.

The instructor then handed out the final exam, which consisted of two sentences. "Congratulations," it read, "you have just received an A in this class. Keep believing in yourself."[8] It was a just reward for the students who had worked hard and believed in themselves.

EXPECTATIONS DETERMINE ACTIONS

Fred Smith Sr., one of my mentors and the author of *Leading with Integrity*, says that a linguist with Wycliffe Bible translators told him that in twenty of the world's most primitive languages, the word for *belief* is the same as the word for *do*. It is only as people become more "sophisticated" that they begin to separate the meaning of one word from the other. That insight is very telling because most people separate belief from action. So how can we bring these two things back together? Through our expectations.

We cannot live in a way that is inconsistent with our expectations for ourselves. It just doesn't happen. I once heard a story that I have not been able to confirm about an aviation pioneer who built a plane the year before the Wright brothers made their historic flight in Kitty Hawk. The plane sat in this inventor's barn because he was afraid to fly it. Maybe it was because it had never been done before. Maybe it was because he expected it to fail—I don't know. It's said that after the news reached him about Orville and Wilbur Wright, the man flew his plane. Before then, he didn't believe in himself enough to take the risk.

There are two kinds of people in this world: those who want to get things done and those who don't want to make mistakes. The Wright brothers were of the first type. The would-be aviation pioneer was of the second. If you're of the first type, then you already expect to believe in yourself and take risks. But what if you're of the second type? There's good news: you can grow.

A story in Robert Schuller's book *Tough Times Never Last, but Tough People Do!* is about Sir Edmund Hillary, who was the first person to reach the summit of Mount Everest along with Tibetan Tenzing Norgay. Prior to his success on Everest, Hillary had been part of another expedition, in which the team not only had failed to reach the summit but also had lost one of its members. At a reception for the expedition members in London, Hillary stood to address the audience. Behind the platform was a huge photograph of Everest. Hillary turned to face the image of the mountain and exclaimed, "Mount Everest, you have defeated us. But I will return. And I will defeat you. *Because you cannot get any bigger, and I can.*"[9]

I don't know what challenges you face. They may be getting bigger every day, or they may already be as big as they can get, like Mount Everest. But I do know this: the only way you can rise to meet the challenges effectively is to expect to. You don't overcome challenges by making them smaller. You overcome them by making yourself bigger!

ACTIONS DETERMINE RESULTS

Results come from actions. That may seem obvious in the physical realm. Sir Isaac Newton's third law of motion states that for every action, there is an equal and opposite reaction. However, in the human realm, many people don't make the connection. They simply hope for good results. Hope is not a strategy. If you want good results, you need to perform good actions. If you want to perform good actions, you must have positive expectations. To have positive expectations, you have to first believe. It all goes back to that. Radio personality Paul Harvey observed, "If you don't live it, you don't believe it." It all starts with belief.

A popular activity for tourists in Switzerland is mountain climbing—not the type of climbing that the world-class mountaineers do to scale the world's highest peaks. Maybe it would be more accurate to call it high-altitude hiking. Groups depart from a "base camp" early in the morning with the intention of making it to the top of the mountain by mid-afternoon.

I talked to a guide about his experiences with these groups, and he described an interesting phenomenon. He said that for most of these expeditions, the group stops at a halfway house where the climbers have lunch, catch their breath, and prepare themselves for the last leg of the rigorous climb. Invariably some members of the group opt for the warmth and comfort of the halfway house and decide not to climb to the top. As the rest of the group leaves, the ones who stay are happy and talkative. It's a party. But when the shadows begin to lengthen, many make their way over to the window that looks up the mountain. And the room gets quiet as they wait for the climbers to return. Why is that? They realize they've missed a special opportunity. Most of them will never be in that part of the world again. They won't ever have a chance to climb that mountain again. They missed it.

That's what it's like when people don't make the most of

their talent, when they don't believe in themselves and their potential, when they don't act on their belief and try to make the most of every opportunity.

Don't allow that to happen to you! Live the life you were meant to. Try to see yourself as you could be, and then do everything in your power to believe that you can become that person. That is the first important step in becoming a successful person.

CHAPTER 3

FIRE UP YOUR PASSION

What carries people to the top? What makes them take risks, go the extra mile, and do whatever it takes to achieve their goals? It isn't talent. It's passion. Passion is more important than a plan. Passion creates fire. It provides fuel. I have yet to meet a passionate person who lacked energy. As long as the passion is there, it doesn't matter if they fail. It doesn't matter how many times they fall down. It doesn't matter if others are against them or if people say they cannot succeed. They keep going and make the most of whatever talent they possess.

YOUR PASSION CAN EMPOWER YOU

Passion can energize every aspect of a person's life—including his talent. Have you ever known a person with great passion who lacked the energy to act on what mattered to her? I doubt it. A passionate person with limited talent will outperform a passive person who possesses greater talent. Why? Because passionate people act with boundless enthusiasm, and they just keep on going!

Authors Robert J. Kriegel and Louis Patler cite a study of fifteen hundred people over twenty years that shows how passion makes a significant difference in a person's career:

> At the outset of the study, the group was divided into Group A, 83 percent of the sample, who were embarking on a career chosen for the prospects of making money now in order to do what they wanted later, and Group B, the other 17 percent of the sample, who had chosen their career path for the reverse reason, they were going to pursue what they wanted to do now and worry about the money later.
>
> The data showed some startling revelations:
>
> - At the end of the twenty years, 101 of the 1,500 had become millionaires.
> - Of the millionaires, all but one—100 out of 101— were from Group B, the group that had chosen to pursue what they loved![1]

The old saying is true: "Find something you like to do so much that you'd gladly do it for nothing, and if you learn to do it well, someday people will be happy to pay you for it." When that's the case, then true are the words of a motto that Dr. Charles Mayo kept on his office wall: "There's no fun like work."

THE POWER OF PASSION

There really is no substitute for passion when it comes to energizing your talent. Take a look at what passion can do for you:

1. Passion Is the First Step to Achievement

Loving what you do is the key that opens the door for achievement. When you don't like what you're doing, it really shows—no matter how hard you try to pretend it doesn't. You can become like the little boy named Eddie whose grandmother was an opera lover. She had season tickets, and when Eddie turned eight, she decided to take him to a performance of Wagner—in German—as his birthday present. The next day, at his mother's prompting, the child wrote the following in a thank-you note: "Dear Grandmother, thank you for the birthday present. It is what I always wanted, but not very much. Love, Eddie."

It's difficult to achieve when you don't have the desire to do so. That's why passion is so important. There is a story about Socrates in which a proud and disdainful young man came to the philosopher and, with a smirk, said, "O great Socrates, I come to you for knowledge."

Seeing the shallow and vain young man for what he was, Socrates led the young man down to the sea into waist-deep water. Then he said, "Tell me again what you want."

"Knowledge," he responded with a smile.

Socrates grabbed the young man by his shoulders and pushed him down under the water, holding him there for thirty seconds. "Now what do you want?"

"Wisdom, O great Socrates," the young man sputtered.

The philosopher pushed him under once again. When he let him up, he asked again, "What do you want?"

"Knowledge, O wise and—" he managed to spit out before Socrates held him under again, this time even longer.

"What do you want?" the old man asked as he let him up again. The younger man coughed and gasped.

"Air!" he screamed. "I need air!"

"When you want knowledge as much as you just wanted air, then you will get knowledge," the old man stated as he returned to shore.

The only way you can achieve anything of significance is to really want it. Passion provides that.

2. PASSION INCREASES WILLPOWER

One of my roles as a motivational teacher is to try to help people reach their potential. For years, I tried to inspire passion in audiences by going about it the wrong way. I used to tell people about what made me passionate, what made me want to get out and do my best. But I could see that it wasn't having the effect I desired—people just didn't respond. I couldn't ignite others' passion by sharing my own.

I decided to change my focus. Instead of sharing my passion, I started helping others discover their passion. To do that, I ask these questions:

What do you sing about?
What do you cry about?
What do you dream about?

The first two questions speak to what touches you at a deep level today. The third answers what will bring you fulfillment tomorrow. The answers to these questions can often help people discover their true passion.

While everybody can possess passion, not everyone takes the time to discover it. And that's a shame. Passion is fuel for the will. Passion turns your have-tos into want-tos. What we accomplish in life is based less on what we want and more on how much we want it. The secret to willpower is what someone once called *wantpower*. People who want something enough usually find the willpower to achieve it.

You can't help people become winners unless they want to win. Champions become champions from within, not from without.

3. PASSION PRODUCES ENERGY

When you have passion, you become energized. You don't have to produce perseverance; it is naturally present in you. It helps you enjoy the journey as much as reaching the destination. Without it, achievement becomes a long and difficult road.

For many years my wife, Margaret, has called me the Energizer Bunny with a nod to those commercials where the battery-operated rabbit keeps going and going. I guess she does so with good reason. I do have a lot of energy. There are always things I hope to do, people I want to see, and goals I want to reach. The reason is passion! We often call people high energy or low energy based on how much they do, but I have come to the conclusion that it might be more appropriate to call them high or low *passion*.

During a Q and A session at a conference, an attendee once asked me, "What is the secret of your passion?" It took me only a moment to be able to articulate it:

1. I am gifted at what I do (strength zone).
2. What I do makes a difference (results).
3. When I do what I was made to do, I feel most alive (purpose).

I believe all passionate people feel that way. Aviation

pioneer Charles Lindbergh observed, "It is the greatest shot of adrenaline to be doing what you've wanted to do so badly. You almost feel like you could fly without the plane."

Some people say that they feel burned out. The truth is that they probably never were on fire in the first place. Writer and editor Norman Cousins said, "Death isn't the greatest loss in life. The greatest loss is what dies inside of us while we live." Without passion, a part of us does becomes dead. And if we're not careful, we could end up like the person whose tombstone read, "Died at thirty. Buried at sixty." Don't allow that to happen to you. Be like Rueben Martinez who is still going strong beyond age sixty. People often describe him as acting half his age. What gives him such energy? His passion!

4. Passion Is the Foundation for Excellence

Passion can transform someone from average to excellent. I can tell you that from experience. When I was in high school, I wasn't a great student. My priorities were basketball first, friends second, and studies a distant third. Why? Because playing basketball and spending time with friends were things I was passionate about. I studied, but only to please my parents. School held little appeal for me.

Everything changed when I went to college. For the first time I was studying subjects that mattered to me. They were interesting, and they would apply to my future career. My grades went up because my passion did. In high school I was sometimes on the principal's "list" (which was not a good thing), but in college I continually made the *dean's* list. Passion fired my desire to achieve with excellence.

Civil rights leader Martin Luther King Jr. asserted, "If a man hasn't discovered something that he will die for, he isn't fit to live."[2] When you find purpose, you find passion. And when you find passion, it energizes your talent so that you can achieve excellence.

5. Passion Is the Key to Success

People are such that whenever anything fires their souls, impossibilities vanish. Perhaps that's why philosopher-poet Ralph Waldo Emerson wrote, "Every great and commanding movement in the annals of the world is the triumph of enthusiasm."

I read about two hundred executives who were asked what makes people successful. The number one quality they cited was enthusiasm, not talent—eighty percent of them recognized that there needed to be a fire within to achieve success.

The most talented people aren't always the ones who win. If they did, how could anyone explain the success of the 1980 U.S. Olympic hockey team, which was depicted in the movie *Miracle*, or the Hall of Fame careers of basketball's Larry Bird or football's Joe Montana? Of Montana, teammate Ronnie Lott said, "You can't measure the size of his heart with a tape measure or a stopwatch." It takes more than talent to create success. It takes passion.

6. Passion in a Person Is Contagious

Writer and promotional publicist Eleanor Doan remarked, "You cannot kindle a fire in any other heart until it is burning within your own." I believe that's true. One of my favorite subjects is communication. I have studied and taught it for years, and I always enjoy observing great communicators in action. I believe that people are instructed by reason, but they are inspired by passion.

Even a brief review of effective leaders and businesspeople throughout history illustrates that their passion "caught on" with others. One of my favorites is Winston Churchill. In the 1930s, Churchill was beginning to fade from view in British politics. But with the rise of Hitler came a rise in Churchill's passion. Long before others did, Churchill spoke out against the Nazis. He had a passion to protect freedom and democracy. And when Hitler declared war and sought to conquer Europe and crush England, Churchill's passion for resistance became infused in the people of Britain and eventually the United States. Without Churchill, the fate of the free world might have turned out to be quite different.

PUTTING YOUR PASSION TO WORK

If you don't possess the energy you desire, then you need to fire up your passion. Here is how I suggest you proceed:

1. PRIORITIZE YOUR LIFE ACCORDING TO YOUR PASSION

People who have passion but lack priorities are like individuals who find themselves in a lonely log cabin deep in the woods on a cold snowy night and then light a bunch of small candles and place them all around the room. They don't create enough light to help them see, nor do they produce enough heat to keep them warm. At best, they merely make the room seem a bit more cheerful. On the other hand, people who possess priorities but no passion are like those who stack wood in the fireplace of that same cold cabin but never light the fire. But people who have passion with priorities are like those who stack the wood, light the fire, and enjoy the light and heat that it produces.

Prioritizing your life according to your passion can be risky. For most people, it requires a major realignment in their work and private lives. But you can't be successful and play it safe. Advertising agency president Richard Edler stated this:

> Safe living generally makes for regrets later on. We are all given talents and dreams. Sometimes the two don't match. But more often than not, we compromise both before ever finding out. Later on, as successful as we might be, we find ourselves looking back longingly to that time when we should have chased our *true* dreams and our *true*[3] talents for all they were worth. Don't let yourself be pressured into thinking that your dreams or your talents aren't prudent. They were never meant to be prudent. They were meant to bring joy and fulfillment into your life.[3]

If your priorities are not aligned with your passion, then begin thinking about making changes in your life. Will change be risky? Probably. But which would you rather live with? The pain of risk or the pain of regret?

2. Protect Your Passion

If you've ever built a fire, then you know this: the natural tendency of fire is to go out. If you want to keep a fire hot, then you need to feed it, and you need to protect it. Not everyone in your life will help you do that when it comes to your passion. In truth, there are two kinds of people: fire*lighters*, who will go out of their way to help you keep your fire hot, and fire*fighters*, who will throw cold water on the fire of passion that burns within you.

How can you tell the firelighters from the firefighters? Listen to what they say. Firefighters use phrases like these:

- "It's not in the budget."
- "That's not practical."
- "We tried that before and it didn't work."
- "We've never done that before."
- "Yeah, but . . ."
- "The boss won't go for it."
- "If it ain't broke, then don't fix it."
- "That's not the way we do things around here."
- "It'll never work."
- "But who will do all the extra work?"
- "You're not _____ [smart, talented, young, old, etc.] enough."
- "You're getting too big for your britches."
- "Who do you think you are?"

If you've heard one or more of these phrases coming from people you know, you may want to create some distance between yourself and them. These firefighters focus on what's wrong rather than what's right. They find the cloud that comes with every silver lining. They doubt. They resist change. They keep people from reaching their potential by trying to put out the fire of their passion. Stay away from them. Instead, spend more time with people who see you not just as you are but as you could be; people who encourage your dreams, ignite your passion. I try to schedule a lunch or two with firelighters like these every month. They really fire me up and energize me to do what I know is best for me.

3. Pursue Your Passion with Everything You've Got

Daniel Eugene "Rudy" Ruettiger, upon whose life the movie *Rudy* was based, observed, "If you really, really believe in your dream, you'll get there. But you have to have passion and total commitment to make it happen. When you have passion and commitment, you don't need a complex plan. Your plan is your life is your dream."[4]

What do you want to accomplish in your lifetime? How do you want to focus your energy: on survival, success, or significance? We live in a time and place with too many opportunities for survival alone. And there's more to life than mere success. We need to dream big. We need to adopt the perspective of someone like playwright George Bernard Shaw, who wrote,

> I am convinced that my life belongs to the whole community; and as long as I live, it is my privilege to do for it whatever I can, for the harder I work the more I live. I rejoice in the life for its own sake. Life is no brief candle to me. It is a sort of splendid torch which I got hold of for a moment, and I want to make it burn as brightly as possible before turning it over to future generations.

Shaw had passion—for life and his work. Your passion has the potential to provide you energy far beyond the limitations of your talent. In the end, you will be remembered for your passion. It is what will energize your talent. It is what will empower you to make your mark.

Chapter 4

Initiate Action

It's a cliché to say that every journey begins with the first step, yet it is still true. Successful people don't wait for everything to be perfect to move forward. They don't wait for all the problems or obstacles to disappear. They don't wait until their fear subsides. They take initiative. They know a secret that good leaders understand—momentum is their friend. As soon as they take action and start moving forward, things become a little easier. If the momentum gets strong enough, many of the problems take care of themselves and talent can take over. But it starts only after you've taken those first steps.

INSIGHTS ON INITIATIVE

If you want to reach your potential, you have to show initiative. Here's why:

1. Initiative Is the First Step to Anywhere You Want to Go

A tourist paused for a rest in a small town in the mountains. He sat down on a bench next to an old man in front of the town's only store. "Hi, friend," he said, "can you tell me something this town is noted for?"

"Well," answered the old man after a moment's hesitation, "you can start here and get to anywhere in the world you want."

That's true of nearly every location. Where you finish in life isn't determined so much by *where* you start as by *whether* you start. If you're willing to get started and keep initiating, there's no telling how far you might go.

That was the case for Les Brown. Les and his brother, Wes, were adopted when they were six weeks old, and they grew up in Liberty City, a poor section of Miami, Florida. As a child, Les was branded a slow learner and given little chance of success by many of his teachers. But with the encouragement of one of his high school teachers, who told him, "Someone else's opinion of you does not have to become your reality," Les managed to graduate from high school and later got a job as a radio DJ. With much hard work, he became a broadcast manager. He got involved in his community, became a community activist and leader, and eventually was elected to the state legislature for three terms. And then he turned his attention to public speaking, where he received the National Speakers Association's highest honor and was named one of the world's top five speakers according to Toastmasters in 1992. He has written books, hosts his own syndicated television show, owns a business, and is in great demand as a public speaker.

When he started life, most people wouldn't have given him much of a chance to succeed. Few thought he had talent.

But he just kept moving forward, and he has since moved far beyond his detractors. Successful people initiate—and they follow through.[1]

2. Initiative Closes the Door to Fear

Author Katherine Paterson said, "To fear is one thing. To let fear grab you by the tail and swing you around is another."[2] We all have fears. The question is whether we are going to control them or allow them to control us.

In 1995, my friend Dan Reiland and his wife, Patti, went skydiving along with a group of friends (including my writer, Charlie Wetzel). They approached the event with a mixture of excitement and fear. At the skydiving center in Southern California, they received only a few minutes of training to prepare them for their tandem jumps. Dan said they were feeling pretty good about the whole thing until a guy walked into the room and made a pitch to sell them life insurance.

As the plane ascended to 11,000 feet, they became increasingly nervous. Then they opened the sliding door at the back of the plane, at which point the fear factor went through the roof. Wishing they had worn rubber pants, they approached the door, each of them harnessed to a jumpmaster, and then launched themselves out of the plane.

Within seconds, they were hurtling toward the earth at 120 miles an hour. And after a free fall of 6,000 feet, they pulled their rip cords. When the canopy opened, with a forceful jolt they went from 120 miles an hour to 25 miles an hour. Dan said, "It made my underwear find places it had never found before!"

I laugh whenever Dan tells the story, but I was really surprised to learn from Dan and Patti that as petrified as they were before they jumped, all their fear was gone the second they left the plane.

Author and pastor Norman Vincent Peale asserted, "Action is a great restorer and builder of confidence. Inaction is not only the result, but the cause, of fear. Perhaps the action you take will be successful; perhaps different action or adjustments will have to follow. But any action is better than no action at all." If you want to close the door on fear, get moving.

3. Initiative Opens the Door to Opportunity

Benjamin Franklin, one of our nation's Founding Fathers, advised, "To succeed, jump as quickly at opportunities as you do at conclusions." People who take initiative and work hard may succeed, or they may fail. But anyone who doesn't take initiative is almost guaranteed to fail.

No one can wait until everything is perfect to act and expect to be successful. It's better to be eighty percent sure and make things happen than it is to wait until you are one hundred percent sure because by then, the opportunity will have already passed you by.

4. Initiative Eases Life's Difficulties

Psychiatrist M. Scott Peck famously stated, "Life is difficult." That's not most people's problem. Their response to life's difficulties is. Too many people wait around for their ship to come in. When they take that approach to life, they often find it to be hardship. The things that simply come to us are rarely the things we want. To have a chance at getting what we desire, we need to work for it.

Philosopher and author William James said, "Nothing is so fatiguing as the hanging on of an uncompleted task." The longer we let things slide, the harder they become. The hardest work is often the accumulation of many easy things that should have been done yesterday, last week, or last month. The only way to get rid of a difficult task is to do it. That takes initiative.

5. Initiative Is Often the Difference Between Success and Failure

A man who was employed by a duke and duchess in Europe was called in to speak to his employer.

"James," said the duchess, "how long have you been with us?"

"About thirty years, Your Grace," he replied.

"As I recall, you were employed to look after the dog."

"Yes, Your Grace," James replied.

"James, that dog died twenty-seven years ago."

"Yes, Your Grace," said James. "What would you like me to do now?"

Like James, too many people are waiting for someone else to tell them what to do next. Nearly all people have good thoughts, ideas, and intentions, but many of them never translate those into action. Doing so requires initiative.

Talent without initiative never reaches its potential. It's like a caterpillar that won't get into its cocoon. It will never transform, forever relegated to crawling on the ground, even though it had the potential to fly.

PEOPLE WHO DON'T INITIATE ACTION

When it comes to initiative, there are really only four kinds of people:

1. People who do the right thing without being told
2. People who do the right thing when told
3. People who do the right thing when told more than once
4. People who never do the right thing, no matter what

Anyone who wants to become successful needs to become the first kind of person. Why doesn't everyone do that? I think there are several reasons.

1. People Who Lack Initiative Fail to See the Consequences of Inaction

King Solomon of ancient Israel is said to have been the wisest person who ever lived. Every time I read Proverbs, which he is believed to have authored, I learn something. In recent years I've enjoyed reading his words in a paraphrase called *The Message*:

> You lazy fool, look at an ant. Watch it closely; let it teach you a thing or two. Nobody has to tell it what to do. All summer it stores up food; at harvest it stockpiles provisions. So how long are you going to laze around doing nothing? How long before you get out of bed? A nap here, a nap there, a day off here, a day off there, sit back, take it easy—do you know what comes next? Just this: You can look forward to a dirt-poor life, poverty your permanent houseguest![3]

British civil servant and economist Sir Josiah Stamp remarked, "It is easy to dodge our responsibilities, but we cannot dodge the consequences of dodging our responsibilities."

2. PEOPLE WHO LACK INITIATIVE WANT
SOMEONE ELSE TO MOTIVATE THEM

Successful people don't need a lighted fuse to motivate them. Their motivation comes from within. If we wait for others to motivate us, what happens when a coach, a boss, or other inspirational person doesn't show up? We need a better plan than that.

Tom Golisano, founder of Paychex, Inc., offered this considered opinion: "I believe you don't motivate people. What you do is hire motivated people, then make sure you don't demotivate them."[4] If you want to get ahead, you need to light your own fire.

3. PEOPLE WHO LACK INITIATIVE LOOK
FOR THE PERFECT TIME TO ACT

Timing is important—no doubt about that. The Law of Timing in my book *The 21 Irrefutable Laws of Leadership* states, "When to lead is as important as what to do and where to go."[5] But it's also true that all worthwhile endeavors in life require risk. I love this Chinese proverb: "He who deliberates fully before taking a step will spend his entire life on one leg." For many people, the tragedy isn't that life ends too soon; it's that they wait too long to begin it.

4. PEOPLE WHO LACK INITIATIVE LIKE
TOMORROW BETTER THAN TODAY

One of the reasons noninitiators have such a difficult time getting started is that they focus their attention on tomorrow instead of today. Jazz musician Jimmy Lyons remarked, "Tomorrow is the only day in the year that appeals to a lazy man." But that attitude gets us into trouble because the only time over which we have any control is the present.

Edgar Guest wrote a poem that captures the fate of those who have this problem. It is appropriately titled "To-morrow":

> He was going to be all that a mortal should be
> To-morrow.
> No one should be kinder or braver than he
> To-morrow.
> A friend who was troubled and weary he knew,
> Who'd be glad of a lift and who needed it, too;
> On him he would call and see what he could do
> To-morrow.
> Each morning he stacked up the letters he'd write
> To-morrow.
> And thought of the folks he would fill with delight
> To-morrow.
> It was too bad, indeed, he was busy to-day,
> And hadn't a minute to stop on his way;
> More time he would have to give others, he'd say
> To-morrow.
> The greatest of workers this man would have been
> To-morrow.
> The world would have known him, had he ever seen
> To-morrow.
> But the fact is he died and he faded from view,
> And all that he left here when living was through
> Was a mountain of things he intended to do
> To-morrow.[6]

The idea of tomorrow can be very seductive, but the promise

that it holds is often false. Spanish priest and writer Baltasar Gracian said, "The wise man does at once what the fool does finally." Anything worth doing is worth doing immediately. Remember that for people who never start, their difficulties never stop.

HOW TO DEVELOP GREATER INITIATIVE

To be honest, all of us are plagued by procrastination in some area of our lives. If something is unpleasant, uninteresting, or complex, we tend to put it off. Even some things we *like* doing can cause us difficulty. Johann Wolfgang von Goethe observed, "To put your ideas into action is the most difficult thing in the world." Yet to reach our potential and become successful, we must show initiative. Here are some suggestions to help you as you strive to help yourself in this area:

1. Accept Responsibility for Your Life

Greek philosopher Socrates said, "To move the world we must first move ourselves." Show me those who neglect to take responsibility for their own lives, and I'll show you people who also lack initiative. Responsibility and initiative are inseparable.

Everyone experiences setbacks. We all face obstacles. From time to time, we all feel that the deck is stacked against us. We need to show initiative anyway. Dick Butler asserted, "Life isn't fair. It isn't going to be fair. Stop sniveling and whining and go out and make it happen for you. In business I see too many people who expect the financial tooth fairy to come at night and remove that ugly dead tooth from under the pillow and substitute profitability just in the nick of time at the end of the fiscal year." There's a saying that great souls have wills but feeble ones have only wishes. We cannot wish our way to success. We need to take responsibility and act.

2. Examine Your Reasons for Not Initiating

Chinese philosopher Mencius made this point: "If your deeds are unsuccessful, seek the reason in yourself. When your own person is correct, the whole world will turn to you." If you lack initiative, the only way you will be able to change is to first identify the specific problem. Think about the reasons people lack initiative already outlined in this chapter. Are you in denial about the consequences of not taking initiative and responsibility for yourself? Are you waiting for others to motivate you instead of working to motivate yourself? Are you waiting for everything to be perfect before you act? Are you fantasizing about tomorrow instead of focusing on what you can do today? Or is there some other issue that is preventing you from taking action?

What's important is that you separate legitimate reasons from excuses. An excuse puts the blame on someone or something outside you. Excuses are like exit signs on the road of progress. They take us off track. Know this: it's easier to move from failure to success than from excuses to success. Eliminate excuses. Once you've done that, you can turn your attention to the reasons—and how to overcome them.

3. Focus on the Benefits of Completing a Task

It is extremely difficult to be successful if you are forever putting things off. Procrastination is the fertilizer that makes difficulties grow. When you take too long to make up your mind about an opportunity that presents itself, you will miss out on seizing it. In the previous chapter I wrote about the importance of aligning your priorities with your passion. To become effective and make progress in your area of talent or responsibility, you can't spend your valuable time on unimportant or unnecessary tasks. So I'm going to make an assumption that if you do procrastinate about a task, it is a necessary one. (If it's not, don't put it off; eliminate it.) To get yourself over the hump, focus on what you'll get out of it if you get it done. Will completing the task bring a financial benefit? Will it clear the way for something else you would *like* to do? Does it represent a milestone in your development or the completion of something bigger? At the very least, does it help to clear the decks for you emotionally? If you seek a positive reason, you are likely to find one.

Once you find that idea, start moving forward and act decisively. U.S. admiral William Halsey observed, "All problems become smaller if you don't dodge them, but confront them. Touch a thistle timidly, and it pricks you; grasp it boldly, and its spines crumble."

4. Share Your Goal with a Friend Who Will Help You

No one achieves success alone. As the Law of Significance states in my book *The 17 Indisputable Laws of Teamwork*, "One is too small a number to achieve greatness."[7] Lindbergh didn't fly solo across the Atlantic without help, Einstein didn't develop the theory of relativity in a vacuum, and Columbus didn't discover the New World on his own. They all had help.

My primary partner in life has been my wife, Margaret. She has been a part of every significant goal I have achieved. She is the first to know when I identify a goal, and she is both the first and the last to support me along the way. And of course, many others have helped me and encouraged me along the way, particularly my parents and my brother, Larry.

In recent years, a key person in supporting me has been John Hull, the president and CEO of EQUIP. When I set the goal of EQUIP to train one million leaders around the globe, the task seemed formidable. As much as I was dedicated to that vision, I had moments when I wondered if it was really possible. John not only was encouraging, but he took ownership of the vision and launched the plan to accomplish it. As you read this book, we have surpassed the goal of training one million leaders and are now working on training another million. One of the reasons I love and admire John is his initiative.

There is no way to put a value on the assistance that others can give you in achieving your dreams. Share your goals and dreams with people who care about you and will encourage and assist you in accomplishing them. It means taking a risk because you will have to be vulnerable in sharing your hopes and ambitions. But the risk is worth taking.

5. Break Large Tasks Down into Smaller Ones

Once you remove some of the internal barriers that may be stopping you from taking initiative and you enlist the help of others, you're ready to get practical. Many times large tasks overwhelm people, and that's a problem because overwhelmed people seldom initiate.

Here's how I suggest you proceed in breaking an intimidating goal into more manageable parts:

Divide it by categories. Most large objectives are complex and can be broken into steps for functions. The smaller pieces often require the effort of people with particular talents. Begin by figuring out what skill sets will be required to accomplish the smaller tasks.

Prioritize it by importance. When we don't take initiative and prioritize what we must do according to its importance, the tasks begin to arrange themselves according to their urgency. When the urgent starts driving you instead of the important, you lose any kind of initiative edge, and instead of activating your talent, it robs you of the best opportunities to use it.

Order it by sequence. Dividing the task according to its categories helps you understand *how* you will need to accomplish it. Prioritizing by importance helps you understand *why* you need to do each part of it. Ordering by sequence helps you know *when* each part needs to be done. The important thing here is to create a timetable, give yourself deadlines, and stick to them. The biggest lie we tell ourselves when it comes to action is, "I'll do it later."

Assign it by abilities. When you divide the large task into smaller ones by category, you begin to understand what kinds of people you'll need to get the job done. At this stage you very specifically answer the *who* question. As a leader, I can tell you that the most important step in accomplishing something big is determining who will be on the team. Assign tasks to winners and give them authority and responsibility, and the job will get done. Fail to give a specific person ownership of the task or give it to an average person, and you may find yourself in trouble.

Accomplish it by teamwork. Even if you break down a task, strategically plan, and recruit great people, you still need one more element to succeed. Everyone has to be able to work together. Teamwork is the glue that can bring it all together.

6. Allocate Specific Times to Tasks
You Might Procrastinate

Dawson Trotman, author and founder of The Navigators, observed, "The greatest time wasted is the time getting started." Haven't you found that to be true? The hardest part of writing a letter is penning the first line. The hardest part of making a tough phone call is picking up the receiver and dialing the number. The most difficult part of practicing the piano is sitting down at the keyboard.

It's the start that often stops people. So how do you overcome that difficulty? Try scheduling a specific time for something you don't like doing. For example, if dealing with difficult people is a regular part of your job, but you tend to avoid doing it, then schedule a set time for it. Maybe the best time would be between two and three o'clock every day. Treat it like an appointment, and when three o'clock rolls around, stop until tomorrow.

7. Remember, Preparation Includes Doing

One of the questions I often hear concerns writing. Young leaders frequently ask me how I got started, and I tell them about my first book, *Think on These Things*. It's a small book comprised of many three-page chapters, but it took me nearly a year to write it. I remember many nights when I spent hours scribbling on a legal pad only to have a few sentences to show for my effort.

"I want to sell a lot of books and influence a lot of people like you do," these young leaders will declare.

"That's great," I'll answer. "What have you written?"

"Well, nothing yet" is typically the response.

"Okay," I say. "What are you working on?" I ask the question hoping to give some encouragement.

"Well, I'm not actually writing yet, but I have a lot of ideas," they'll say, explaining that they hope they'll have more time next month or next year or after they get out of school. When I hear an answer like that, I know it will never happen. Writers write. Composers compose. Leaders lead. You must take action in order to become who you desire to be. Novelist Louis L'Amour, who wrote more than a hundred books and sold more than 230 million copies, advised, "Start writing, no matter about what. The water does not flow until the faucet is turned on."

Desire isn't enough. Good intentions aren't enough. Talent isn't enough. Success requires initiative. Michael E. Angier, founder of SuccessNet, stated, "Ideas are worthless. Intentions have no power. Plans are nothing . . . unless they are followed with action. Do it now!"

Chapter 5

Focus Your Energy

Watch small children playing, and what do you see? They move quickly from one toy to another and from activity to activity. They expend tremendous amounts of energy but get little done. That's to be expected. They are exploring their world and learning by doing.

Focusing our energy does not come naturally to us, yet it is essential for anyone who wants to make the most of his talent. Having talent without focus is like being an octopus on roller skates. You can be sure that there will be plenty of movement, but you won't know in what direction it will be. Talent with focus directs you and has the potential to take you far.

THE POWER OF FOCUSED ENERGY

Focusing can bring tremendous power. Without it, you will often feel drained and unable to accomplish much. With it, you will find that your talents and abilities gain direction and intentionality. And those qualities pay off by producing results.

Here are some facts you need to know about focus:

1. Focus Does Not Come Naturally to Most People

We live in a culture with almost infinite choices and opportunities, and because of that, most people find themselves pulled in dozens of directions. What's worse is that people often find themselves expending much of their time and energy on things they don't really care about. Don Marquis, author of *Archy and Mehitabel*, put it this way: "Ours is a world where people don't know what they want and are willing to go through hell to get it."

The solution to such a predicament is focus. Poet William Matthews wrote, "One well-cultivated talent, deepened and enlarged, is worth one hundred shallow faculties. The first law of success in this day, when so many things are clamoring for attention, is concentration—to bend all the energies to one point, and to go directly to that point, looking neither to the right nor to the left."[1]

I try to maintain my focus in the moment by heeding the advice of the martyred missionary Jim Elliott, who said, "Wherever you are, be all there." But I also look at the bigger picture. As a leader, I am always asking myself, *Am I helping others make progress?* I am vigilant about how I spend my time, with whom I am spending it, how it fits into the bigger picture, and whether it produces results. And my assistant, Linda Eggers, also keeps me on track by overseeing my calendar. She is a tremendous asset for helping me maintain my priorities. If I feel that I'm not moving forward and helping others throughout the day, then I know I'm off track in some way. Linda helps me monitor that.

2. FOCUS INCREASES YOUR ENERGY

If you desire to achieve something, you first need to know what your target is. That's true even when it comes to personal development. If you lack focus, you will be all over the place. Attempting everything, like attempting nothing, will suck the life out of you. It will sap you of energy and new opportunities. And whatever momentum you have going for you will be diminished.

In contrast, focus gives you energy. Polar explorer Admiral Richard E. Byrd asserted, "Few men during their lifetime come anywhere near exhausting the resources dwelling within them. There are deep wells of strength that are never used."[2] One of the reasons those wells often go untapped is lack of focus. Something wonderful happens when we narrow our focus and set goals. That is where the real magic starts. The mind doesn't reach toward achievement until it has clear objectives.

After American astronauts successfully landed on the moon, Albert Siepert, deputy director of the Kennedy Space Center, attributed their success, at least in part, to NASA's focus. For a decade, the organization put nearly all of its time and energy into reaching the moon. Siepert observed, "The reason NASA has succeeded is because NASA had a clear-cut goal and expressed its goal. By doing this, we drew the best of men to our goal and the support of every phase of government to reach our goal."

3. FOCUS LIFTS YOU

Scholar and educator David Star Jordan said, "The world stands aside to let anyone pass who knows where he or she is going." In a sea of mediocrity, just knowing what you want to do and then making an effort to pursue it distinguishes you from almost everybody else.

The plainspoken American writer Henry David Thoreau asked, "Did you ever hear of a man who had striven all his life faithfully and singly toward an object, and in no measure obtained it? If a man constantly aspires, is he not elevated?" Focus always has an impact. Just by striving to become better than you are, you become elevated—even if you don't accomplish what you desire, and even if others *don't* step aside for you. You can't shoot for the stars and remain unaffected by the effort.

4. FOCUS EXPANDS YOUR LIFE

A few years ago I wrote a book called *Thinking for a Change* in which I described the various thinking skills that can help a person become more successful. Included was a chapter on focused thinking, the ability to remove distractions and mental clutter so that a person can concentrate with clarity. In it I explained how I often bring together a team of people to help me brainstorm when working on a project. Because we focus our attention on the subject at hand, we are able to expand ideas in a way that we wouldn't be able to do otherwise.

Mike Kendrick asserts, "What you focus on expands." That may seem ironic, but it's true. Have you noticed that if you consider buying a particular kind of car, you begin seeing them everywhere? Narrowing your view widens your perspective. On the other hand, if you actually try to expand your view, instead of taking more in, it simply wears you out. If you want to expand your capacity, then focus.

5. FOCUS MUST BE INTENTIONALLY SUSTAINED

People do not naturally remain focused. Just as light naturally loses its focus and gets diffused, so does a person's attention. It takes a lot of effort, but the payoff is significant. Hall of Fame baseball player Hank Aaron said, "I think what separates a superstar from the average ballplayer is that he concentrates just a little bit longer." Aaron demonstrated that he was able to sustain his concentration. For thirty-three years, he held the Major League Baseball record for the most home runs hit in a career.

In his book *Laughter, Joy, and Healing*, Donald E. Demaray wrote about a young journalist who was receiving tough criticism from his father because he didn't seem to be making much progress in his career. Undaunted, the young man wrote back to his father explaining that he had a plan for success upon which he was focused. His intentions were as follows:

- At thirty, he would be a great newspaper reporter.
- At forty, he would be a great editor.
- At fifty, he would be a great story writer.
- At sixty, he would be a great fiction writer.
- At seventy, he would be a great grandfather.
- At eighty, he would be a great admirer of beautiful women.
- At ninety, he would be a great loss to the community.

Demaray said that the father got a good laugh from the letter and was gratified when he began to see that his son's career was progressing along those lines.[3]

Several years ago I memorized a definition of success to

help me in my career: "Success is the progressive realization of a predetermined worthwhile goal." What I learned most from that definition is that success is not an event; it is a process. And anytime you engage in a process that takes time, focus is essential. Only people capable of remaining focused can expect to direct their talent and achieve a level of success.

HOW TO INCREASE YOUR FOCUS

If you desire to become successful, you need to make focus your friend. Here's how:

1. BE INTENTIONAL—MAKE EVERY ACTION COUNT

A family who had moved to a new neighborhood got a late start one morning, and as a result their six-year-old missed her bus to school. Though it would make him late for work, the father agreed to take her to school if she could give him directions.

They left their neighborhood, and the young girl began directing her father to take one turn after another. Following twenty minutes of circuitous driving, they arrived at the school, which turned out to be only eight blocks away. Steaming, the father asked the kindergartener why she had him drive all over the place when the school was so close to home.

"We went the way the bus goes," she said. "That's the only way I know."

If you want to maximize your talent and be successful, you need to make every action count. You must determine where you want to go and how to get there. You cannot be like Alice in Lewis Carroll's *Through the Looking Glass*, who asks for directions in this way during her encounter with the Cheshire Cat:

> "Would you tell me please, which way ought I to go from here?" she asks.
>
> "That depends a good deal on where you want to get," the cat replies with a grin.
>
> "I don't care much where," she answers.
>
> "Then it doesn't matter which way you go," the cat responds.[4]

People who are undecided about what they want to do or where they want to go cannot tap into their strength of will—or their talent. As a result, they will merely drift along.

Private investigator and author Bill Copeland advises, "You've removed most of the roadblocks to success when you know the difference between motion and direction." Have you asked yourself what you really want to do? And have you determined that you will pursue it against the odds, despite the obstacles, and regardless of the circumstances? Being intentional is about focusing on doing the right things, moment by moment, day to day, and then following through with them in a consistent way. As President John F. Kennedy asserted, "Efforts and courage are not enough without purpose and direction."

2. Challenge Your Excuses

A sign on the desk of an officer who works at the Pentagon reads, "The secrecy of my job does not permit me to know what I'm doing." It's a clever joke, but it's not funny when it's actually true. People who don't know what they're doing soon become frustrated.

We all have reasons for not doing what we ought to do. We don't have enough time. We don't have enough resources. We don't have enough help. We have problems. We have short-comings. We have distractions. Should we let these things get us off track? No!

3. Don't Let Yesterday Hijack Your Attention

Humorist and entertainer Will Rogers shared this thought: "Don't let yesterday take up too much of today." I've never known a person focusing on yesterday who had a better tomorrow. Too many people *yearn* for the past and get stuck in it. Instead, they should *learn* from the past and let go of it.

Alvin Dark, who was once the manager of the Kansas City Athletics, used to say, "There's no such thing as taking a pitcher out. There's only bringing another pitcher in." That runs contrary to what you hear during most baseball broadcasts, but here's the point. When you say you're going to take a pitcher out, you're probably focused on the mistakes he made—the players he walked, the hits he allowed. That doesn't help you win the game. In contrast, when you say you're putting a pitcher in, you are focusing on what that new pitcher is going to do now to try to help you beat the other team. That can make a big difference in your team's attitude—and in the players' ability to succeed.

Editor and publisher Elbert Hubbard wrote,

A retentive memory may be a good thing, but the ability to forget is the true token of greatness. Successful people forget. They know the past is irrevocable. They're running a race.

They can't afford to look behind. Their eye is on the finish line. Magnanimous people forget. They're too big to let
little things disturb them. They forget easily. If anyone does
them wrong, they consider the source and keep cool. It's only
the small people who cherish revenge. Be a good forgetter.
Business dictates it, and success demands it.[5]

If you desire to make the most of your talent and achieve
success, then you need to make what you're doing now your
focus. Striving for achievements is a lot like driving a car. It's a
good idea to check your rearview mirror occasionally, but not
to give it your complete attention. If you do, you will eventually be incapable of moving forward at all.

4. FOCUS ON THE PRESENT

Just as you should keep your focus off yesterday, you
shouldn't have it on tomorrow. If you're always thinking about
tomorrow, then you'll never get anything done today. Your
focus needs to remain in the one area where you have some
control—today. What's ironic is that if you focus on today, you
get a better tomorrow.

I try to do certain things every day to help me in this area.
I read daily to grow in my personal life. I listen to others
daily to broaden my perspective. I spend time thinking daily
to apply what I am learning. And I try to write daily so that I
can remember what I've learned. I also try to share those lessons with others. (Today's lessons become tomorrow's books.)
Every day I read aloud to myself the daily dozen list from
my book *Today Matters* to help me focus and have the right
mind-set.

You should do something similar. You can't change

yesterday. You can't count on tomorrow. But you can choose what you do today. Giving it your focus will pay dividends.

5. STAY FOCUSED ON RESULTS

Anytime you concentrate on the difficulty of the work at hand instead of its results or rewards, you're likely to become discouraged. Dwell on the difficulties too long and you'll start to develop self-pity instead of self-discipline, and your attention will become scattered instead of focused. As a result, you will accomplish less and less. By focusing on results, you will find it easier to stay positive and encouraged.

Another thing that can distract you from results is inter-action with difficult people. You will come in contact with a lot of people who can impact your efforts as you work on achieving your dreams—some in a negative way. Here are five types of people you are likely to encounter:

- *Refreshers*—they inspire your dreams and energize your talents.
- *Refiners*—they sharpen your ideas and clarify your vision.
- *Reflectors*—they mirror your energy, neither adding nor subtracting from it.
- *Reducers*—they try to reduce your vision and efforts to their comfort level.
- *Rejecters*—they deny your talent, hinder your efforts, and impede your vision.

If you remain focused on results, you will stay grounded. The praise of others is less likely to go to your head, and the negative impact of people such as the reducers and rejecters will be minimized.

6. Develop and Follow Your Priorities

There's an old saying that if you chase two rabbits, both will escape. Unfortunately that is what many people seem to do. They don't focus their attention, and as a result, they become ineffective. Perhaps the reason is that people in our culture have too many choices—nearly unlimited options. Management expert Peter Drucker recognized this phenomenon. He said, "Concentration is the key to economic results. No other principle of effectiveness is violated as constantly today as the basic principle of concentration. . . . Our motto seems to be, 'Let's do a little bit of everything.'"[6]

If you want to develop your talent, you need to focus. If you're going to focus, you need to work on knowing what your true priorities are and then following them. This is something I have learned to do over time. I love options. I like to have the freedom to pursue the best course of action at any given moment. When I was in my twenties, I spent a lot of time doing things that had little return. In my thirties, I did better, but I still wasn't as focused as I should have been. It wasn't until I reached forty that I started to become highly selective about where I spent my time and energy. Today, as I approach sixty, I filter just about everything I do through my top priority: *Am I adding value to people?* For me, it all comes down to that.

7. Focus on Your Strengths, Not Your Weaknesses

There's a story about a couple who bought a new piece of property upon which they intended to establish a farm.

It was good land, and they could hardly wait to move there and get started. As they made plans for the move one night, they began to argue about what to do first. The wife wanted to build the house first. After all, once they moved, the new property would be their home. The husband, who had grown up working on a farm, wanted to build the barn first to house their animals. They went back and forth for a while until the man finally said, "Look, we have to build the barn first—because the barn will build the house, and the garage, the silo, the kids' swing set, and everything else!" When you focus on your priorities and put first things first, everything else is more likely to fall into place.

Anthony Campolo, professor emeritus of sociology at Eastern University in Pennsylvania, says,

> What you commit yourself to will change what you are and make you into a completely different person. Let me repeat that. Not the past but the future conditions you, because what you commit yourself to become determines what you are—more than anything that ever happened to you yesterday or the day before. Therefore, I ask you a very simple question: What are your commitments? Where are you going? What are you going to be? You show me somebody who hasn't decided, and I'll show you somebody who has no identity, no personality, no direction.[7]

Focusing on weaknesses instead of strengths is like having a handful of coins—a few made of pure gold and the rest of tarnished copper—and setting aside the gold coins to spend all your time cleaning and shining the copper ones in the hopes of making them look more valuable. No matter how long you spend on them, they will never be worth what the gold ones are. Go with your greatest assets; don't waste your time.

8. DELAY REWARDS UNTIL THE JOB IS DONE

One of the tricks I've used with myself for years is to reward myself when I've done something that I ought to do. My father taught me that when I was a kid—pay now and play later. I think too often people want the rewards before the results, and for that reason they don't stay as focused as they could.

One secret of a life well lived is making every action count—being intentional. That kind of focus helps people live without regrets because it directs and makes the most of their talent and their opportunities. If you know that you have talent, and you are energetic and active, but you don't see concrete results, then lack of focus is likely your problem. It takes ability plus focus to reach your potential and become the person you desire to be.

Chapter 6

Value Preparation

What happens when you don't prepare? Things you hoped *wouldn't* happen do happen—and they occur with greater frequency than the things you hoped *would* happen. The reason is simple: being unprepared puts you out of position. Ask negotiators what happens at the bargaining table when they are out of position. Ask athletes what happens when they are out of position. They lose. Preparation positions people correctly, and it is often the separation between winning and losing. Successful people who prepare well live by this motto: "All's well that begins well."

WHY PEOPLE FAIL TO PREPARE

Successful people recognized that spectacular achievement comes from unspectacular preparation. Talent wants to jump into action, but preparation positions talent to be effective.

In hindsight, it's easy to recognize the value of preparation. So why do so many people fail to prepare?

They Fail to See the Value of Preparation Before Action

Authors Don Beveridge Jr. and Jeffrey P. Davidson believe that lack of preparation is the primary reason for business failure today. "Poorly educated, poorly prepared, and poorly trained people fail because they do not have the skills or expertise to perform," they say. "Inadequate financing, the number-one reason businesses fail, can also be traced to lack of preparation."[1]

In the introduction to this book I wrote about how talent early in life or in the beginning of a career makes a person stand out—but only for a short time. Why? Talent may be a given, but success you must earn. Proverbs 18:16 states, "A man's gift makes room for him."[2] In other words, your talent will give you an opportunity. But you must remember that the room it makes is only temporary.

Preparation is a major key to achieving any kind of success. It alone can position your talent to achieve its potential. Military people know this. General Douglas MacArthur said, "Preparedness is the key to success and victory." He also stated it more bluntly: "The more you sweat in peace, the less you bleed in war." The actions of Meriwether Lewis demonstrated that he had a similar attitude. Despite all the dangers and deprivations, the brutal weather and hostile Native Americans, Lewis lost only one member of his party, Sergeant Charles Floyd, probably from peritonitis cause by a ruptured appendix. No preparation on Lewis's part could have saved Floyd from that. In fact, in 1804, Floyd probably would have died under the care of a trained physician.

They Fail to Appreciate the Value of Discipline

It's been said that discipline is doing what you really *don't want* to do so that you can do what you really *do want* to do.

Meriwether Lewis's most evident weakness was a tendency to be a bit rash and take offense. In fact, one of Jefferson's serious concerns was that Lewis might alienate the Native Americans and either start a war or get himself and his party killed. Lewis came close several times, including a tense standoff with the Teton Sioux. The explorers were one wrong move away from being wiped out and becoming little more than an obscure footnote in American history. What saved the day? Ambrose says Lewis's rashness was compensated by his tremendous self-discipline. With guns loaded and aimed and dozens of arrows pointed in their direction, Lewis waited out the situation. Eventually a Sioux chief managed to get the angry braves to stand down and defuse the conflict. Lewis understood the value of discipline.

A frustrating thing about preparation is that it usually takes much more time than the actual event one prepares for. Musicians may practice many hours preparing to perform a three-minute piece. Stage actors practice for weeks to prepare for a performance that lasts two hours. I know that when I create a leadership lesson that may take me less than an hour to deliver, it usually takes me eight to ten hours to write it. Discipline is required to keep preparing long hours for something that will be over quickly.

Alexander Hamilton, a Founding Father of the United States and its first secretary of the treasury, said, "Men give me credit for genius; but all the genius I have lies in this: When I have a subject on hand I study it profoundly." Hamilton was a disciplined and highly productive man. He understood that no matter your circumstances, resources, or natural talent, certain things were always within your control—your ability to work harder and smarter than anybody else. That bears remembering as you prepare yourself for the challenges that lie ahead of you.

PREPARATION PRINCIPLES

Automaker Henry Ford observed, "Before everything else, getting ready is the secret of success." Ford understood the power of preparation and all the things it can do for someone:

1. Preparation Allows You to Tap into Your Talent

While I was working on my book *Beyond Talent*, I was scheduled to make a trip to Latin America to teach leadership and meet national leaders in Guatemala, El Salvador, Honduras, Panama, Venezuela, Bolivia, and Peru. I would be gone more than ten days, so before I left I spent an entire day making sure I had the materials I would need to keep working on the book. I reviewed the chapter outlines, gave some thinking time to the subject of the first couple of chapters, and pulled quotes and other materials from my files to take with me. And of course I packed several new legal pads!

I also wrote the book's introduction. A group of excellent leaders and thinkers would be accompanying me on the trip, and I wanted their comments on the direction I was taking the book. I had copies made of that introduction so that I could hand them out to my fellow travelers, and I asked everyone to give me feedback and ideas. (I'm a strong believer in teamwork when related to talent too. I'll write more about that in chapter 14.) And since we spent a lot of hours flying on a plane, during much of that time I pulled out the materials I had packed and did some writing.

As the trip concluded and we were flying back home, one of my travel mates, David McLendon, said to me, "I've learned a valuable lesson on this trip. You came prepared to maximize your time because you knew what you wanted to accomplish. While the rest of us read and talked, you got a lot of work done. You outlined two chapters. You even engaged all of us in the writing of your book!"

What he observed was possible because I had prepared. "You know, David," I replied, "I've found that every minute spent in preparation saves ten in execution." And that had been the case here. Because I spent a day preparing, I was able to work for ten days on that trip. It's not difficult; it just takes planning. The questions I ask myself before a trip like this are really very simple:

- *What work is to be done?*
- *How is it to be done?*
- *When is it to be done?*
- *Where is it to be done?*
- *How fast can it be done?*
- *What do I need to get it done?*

Answering these questions prepares me for what lies ahead. And when I am prepared, my talent is positioned for maximum effect.

2. PREPARATION IS A PROCESS, NOT AN EVENT

We live in a quick-fix society. We think in terms of events and instant solutions. But preparation doesn't work that way. Why? Because it's about you. Anything having to do with people is process-oriented. The Law of Process in *The*

21 Irrefutable Laws of Leadership states, "Leadership develops daily, not in a day." The same can be said of maximizing your talent.

Legendary UCLA basketball coach John Wooden said that the best way to improve your team is to improve yourself. He learned that lesson from his father, Joshua Wooden, who used to tell young John, "Don't try to be better than somebody else, but never cease trying to be the best you can be." That's good advice whether you're playing basketball, parenting, or conducting business.

In 1983, I began teaching and recording monthly leadership lessons. Today, nearly four decades later, I am still teaching them, and I have produced more than three hundred different leadership lessons. How was I able to do it? By continually feeding my mind and adding to my pool of resources. Every day I read and file quotes, stories, and idea starters. Every month I draw upon those filed resources. Every year I use some of those lessons to write new books. My productivity comes more from my preparation than anything else. That positions whatever talent I have so that I can use it to my maximum potential. It is an ongoing process. And if the daily learning and preparation ever stop, so will my productivity.

3. Preparation Precedes Opportunity

There's an old saying: "You can claim to be surprised once; after that, you're unprepared." If you want to take advantage of opportunities to use your talent, then you *must* be prepared when the opportunities arise. Once the opportunity presents itself, it's too late to get ready.

If you study the lives of dynamic men and women, you will find that preparation for opportunity is a common theme.

President Abraham Lincoln said, "I will prepare and someday my chance will come." Prime Minister Benjamin Disraeli of England remarked, "The secret of success in life is for a man to be ready for his time when it comes." Oprah Winfrey asserted, "Luck is a matter of preparation meeting opportunity." And President John F. Kennedy observed, "The time to repair the roof is when the sun is shining." All of these people had talent, prepared themselves, and then made the most of their opportunities when they arose. Many people believe their greatest barrier to opportunity is having one, but the reality is that their greatest barrier is being ready when one arrives.

4. Preparation for Tomorrow Begins with the Right Use of Today

Recently a few friends and I were privileged to have dinner with former New York City mayor Rudy Giuliani and his wife, Judith, in Orlando after a speaking engagement. I found the mayor to be a very warm and personable man who was an easy conversationalist. During our conversation, I of course asked him about his experience during 9/11. He talked about his impressions from that day and how the event impacted him as a leader. He said that leaders need to be ready for anything. They need to study, acquire skills, and plan for every kind of situation.

"Your success will be determined by your ability to prepare," he said. He went on to explain that when a situation like that on September 11 occurs—for which there was no plan in place—leaders must take action and rely on whatever preparation had taken place. In his case, it was the emergency drills they had followed. Both helped during the crisis.

Preparation doesn't begin with what you do. It begins with

what you believe. If you believe that your success tomorrow depends on what you do today, then you will treat today differently. What you receive tomorrow depends on what you believe today. If you are *preparing* today, chances are, you will not be *repairing* tomorrow.

5. Preparation Requires Maintaining Good Perspective

When I was a kid, my first love was basketball. From the time I was ten until I graduated from high school, I was shooting hoops at every free moment. One thing I still enjoy about basketball is how quickly one player can change the tempo and momentum of a game. That's true not only of the stars and starters but also of the players who come off the bench. That's why the "sixth man," the player of starting caliber who is often the first substitute in the game, is so important. Former Boston Celtics coach Tom Heinsohn observed, "The sixth man has to be so stable a player that he can instantly pick up the tempo or reverse it. He has to be able to go in and have an immediate impact. The sixth man has to have the unique ability to be in a ball game while he is sitting on the bench." What makes the sixth man capable of that? Perspective. He has to have both a coach's mind-set as he watches the game from the bench and a player's ability once he steps into it. If he does, then he is prepared to impact the game.

Howard Coonley, the executive after whom the American National Standards Institute named its award honoring service to the national economy, stated, "The executive of the future will be rated by his ability to anticipate his problems rather than to meet them as they come." Perspective not only helps people prepare, but it can also *motivate* them to prepare. I love the quote from Abraham Lincoln, who said, "If I had eight hours to chop down a tree, I'd spend six sharpening my ax." Lincoln had split rails with an ax as a young man, so he knew the value of a sharp ax. Perspective always prompted him to prepare—whether he was getting ready to cut wood, study law on his own to pass the bar, or lead the country.

6. GOOD PREPARATION LEADS TO ACTION

What value has preparation if it never leads to action? Very little. As William Danforth, former chancellor of Washington University in St. Louis, noted, "No plan is worth the paper it is printed on unless it starts you going."

People who enjoy preparation sometimes find themselves caught in the trap of overpreparing, and they sometimes do so to the point that they fail to act. Kathleen Eisenhardt, professor of management science and engineering at Stanford University, studied the decision-making process at twelve technology companies. She found that the fast deciders, who took two to four months to make major decisions, were much more effective than their slower counterparts who wanted to get all the facts of their situation and create consensus. The slower group took up to eighteen months to plan and decide, and by the time they did find resolution, the decision they made was often irrelevant.[3]

Preparation does not mean mastery of the facts. It does not mean knowing all the answers. It does not necessarily mean achieving consensus. (Former British prime minister Margaret Thatcher remarked that "consensus is the negation of leadership.") It means putting yourself in a better position to succeed.

PREPARATION LESSONS FROM GOLF

Sports have always been an area in which you can see the value of preparation. It doesn't matter what sport—good athletes talk about it all of the time. Tennis champion Arthur Ashe explained, "One important key to success is self-confidence. An important key to self-confidence is preparation." Quarterback Joe Namath said simply, "What I do is prepare myself until I know I can do what I have to do."

Friend and fellow golfer Rick Bizet once told me that his golf coach taught him that the only thing that relieves pressure is preparation. If you want to see that preparation in action, observe any professional golfer's pre-shot routine. I particularly appreciate the routine of professional golfer Tom Kite. It contains three main steps: assessment, alignment, and attitude. In fact, I use it as a guideline, not only when playing golf, but also in other situations when I need to prepare myself. I believe you can do the same.

1. ASSESSMENT—AM I EVALUATING CORRECTLY?

Good preparation always begins with assessment. If you don't accurately evaluate where you need to go and what it will take to get there, then you're likely to get into trouble. In golf, good players typically ask themselves these questions to assist in the assessment process:

- **Where do I need to go?** The process begins with finding the right target. That target must be appropriate to your talent. You don't want to be like the Miss America contestant that Jay Leno quoted as saying, "My goal is to bring peace to the entire world—and to get my own apartment."

- **How far is my goal?** Next, a person needs to assess the distance. I enjoy telling my fellow golfers that I have a great short game—but unfortunately only off the tee! It may sound obvious, but you've got to know the distance to your goal to have a shot at making it there.

- **What are the conditions?** Good golfers always take the wind into account. The conditions make all the difference in the world. One of my personal highlights related to golf was the opportunity to play at St. Andrews in Scotland. And I shot really well that day—a 79. How did I do it? There was no wind! My caddie told me, "It's a whole different game with the wind."

- **What will it take to get there?** The final step in the assessment process is knowing what club to use. Gary Player says that bad club selection is the number one error of amateurs. They hit the ball short. It's important to know your skills and limitations when making your assessment.

How would I translate these questions for non-golfing situations? I'd say that you need to know *what* exactly you should be doing; what it will *cost* you in time, effort, and resources to get there; what *obstacles* you are likely to face; and what your *personal limitations* are. If you know these things, you will be well on your way to preparing yourself to achieve your goals.

2. ALIGNMENT—AM I LINED UP CORRECTLY?

A good golfer can conduct the assessment process flawlessly and still miss his or her target horribly. How? By lining up poorly. A well-known psychologist once said, "What is the use of climbing the ladder of success only to find that it's leaning against the wrong building?"

When I first started playing golf, I tried to teach myself the game. I held the club with a baseball grip and lined up in a baseball stance, and more often than not, if I hit the ball any distance, I sent it into the woods. To improve my game, I had to change the way I played golf. I had to relearn the game, and that meant getting help.

If you want to take your game to the next level—personally, professionally, relationally, or recreationally—you need to find someone who is better than you to help you with the preparation process. Be open and honest with that person, and he or she will be able to evaluate your "alignment" and help you get on course.

3. Attitude—Am I Visualizing Correctly?

The final step after assessment and alignment is attitude. In golf, after you select a target and line it up, it's really a mental game. You're not just training your body—you're training your mind. But that's true for any endeavor. You have to believe in yourself and what you're doing. You have to be able to see yourself doing it with your mind's eye. If you can't imagine it, you probably will not be able to achieve it.

Preparation is one of the most obvious choices you must make in order to maximize your talent and become successful. Sometimes the preparation process is long and slow. It may require formal education. It may necessitate your finding wise mentors. It may mean getting out of your comfort zone. Or it could mean simply fine-tuning a skill you've nearly mastered. But whatever it requires, remember that you must be ready when your time comes. People don't get a second chance to seize a once-in-a-lifetime opportunity.

Chapter 7

Embrace Practice

I t is a fact: you play at the level at which you practice. Consistently good practice leads to consistently good play. It sharpens your talent. Successful people understand this. They value practice and develop the discipline to do it. If you want to sum up what lifts most successful individuals above the crowd, you could do it with four little words: *a little bit more*. Successful people pay their dues and do all that is expected of them—plus a little bit more.

THE POWER OF PRACTICE

There's a myth about highly talented people—it's that they are simply born that way. But the truth is that no people reach their potential unless they are willing to practice their way there. Recently I was traveling with Tom Mullins, a former football coach who wrote *The Leadership Game*, which contains successful leadership principles he gleaned from interviewing eight college national champion football coaches. As I talked about the idea of practice with him, he nearly leaped out of his seat. When Tom talks about anything related to leadership, it's like he's back in the locker room talking to his team at halftime when they're two touchdowns behind. I mean, he gets excited!

"Let me tell you, John," he said, "all the national champion coaches told me the key to going from good to great came in two areas: the preparation of the team and the practice of the players. They were forever upgrading their preparation and sharpening their practices." That made sense to me because preparation positions talent and practice sharpens it.

Before we go any further, there are three things you need to know about practice:

1. PRACTICE ENABLES DEVELOPMENT

How do we grow and develop? Through practice. People refine old skills and acquire new ones through practice. That is where the tension between where we are and where we ought to be propels us forward.

Former pro basketball player and U.S. senator Bill Bradley says that he attended a summer basketball camp when he was fifteen years old. There former college and pro basketball star "Easy" Ed Macauley told him, "Just remember that if you're not working at your game to the utmost of your ability, there will be someone out there somewhere with equal ability who will be working to the utmost of his ability. And one day you'll play each other, and he'll have the advantage."

If you desire to improve and develop, then you must practice. It allows you to break your own records and outstrip what you did yesterday. Done correctly, practice keeps making you better than you were yesterday. If you don't practice, you shortchange your potential.

2. Practice Leads to Discovery

In one of Charles Schulz's *Peanuts* strips, Charlie Brown laments to his friend Linus, "Life is just too much for me. I've been confused from the day I was born. I think the whole trouble is that we're thrown into life too fast. We're not really prepared."

"What did you want," Linus responds, "a chance to warm up first?"

We may not get a chance to warm up before entering childhood, but we *can* warm up by practicing the many activities we pursue once life has begun. And it is often during these "warm-ups" that we learn valuable things about ourselves. If you commit yourself to practice, here are a few things you are likely to learn:

Your performance can always be improved. Consultant and author Harvey Mackay says, "A good leader understands that anything that has been done in a particular way for a given amount of time is being done wrong. Every single performance can be improved." Since there is always a better way, your job is to find it.

There's value in starting with small things. Human relations expert Dale Carnegie advised, "Don't be afraid to give your best to what seemingly are small jobs. Every time you conquer one it makes you that much stronger. If you do little things well, the big ones tend to take care of themselves." As you first start to practice, the gains you make may be small. But they will grow. They compound like interest.

Very small differences, consistently practiced, produce results. A curious thing happens when you practice. At first the gains are small, as I said. Then they begin to grow. But there comes a time, if you persevere, when the gains become small again. However, at this season these small gains make big differences. In the Olympics, for example, the difference between the gold medalist and the athletes who finish without a medal is often just hundredths of a second.

A price must be paid to reach the next level. One of the things you often learn in practice is what it will cost to reach a goal or go to the next level. As you get ready to practice, I recommend that you abide by the Taxicab Principle, which is something I learned traveling overseas: before you get into the cab, find out how much the ride is going to cost. If you don't, you may end up paying much more than the ride is worth! As you practice, keep in mind the words of screenwriter Sidney Howard, who remarked, "One half of knowing what you want is knowing what you must give up before you get it."

Many people regard practice as an essentially negative experience. It doesn't have to be that way. The best way to make practice exciting is to think of it in terms of discovery and development.

3. Practice Demands Discipline

One reason some people see practice as a grind is that it requires discipline. Even activities with intense physical demands also require lots of mental discipline. Bill McCartney, former national championship head football coach of the Colorado Buffaloes, used to tell me, "Mental preparation to physical preparation is four to one."

Developing discipline always begins with a struggle. There is no easy way to become a disciplined person. It has nothing to do with talent or ability. It is a matter not of conditions but of choice. But once the choice is made and practice becomes a habit, two things become obvious. The first is a separation between the person who practices and the one who doesn't. The second thing that emerges is a winning spirit. The harder you work, the harder it becomes to surrender.

Greek philosopher Aristotle observed, "Excellence is an art won by training and habituation. We do not act rightly because we have virtue or excellence, but we rather have those because we have acted rightly. We are what we repeatedly do. Excellence, then, is not an act, but a habit." That habit is developed during practice.

THE FIVE PILLARS OF PRACTICE

I talked to a lot of leaders and coaches about practice while I was working on this chapter. And each one of them had a little different take on how to approach practice effectively. Warren Bottke is a PGA master professional who has helped thousands of amateurs and professionals improve their golf game. As Warren and I talked, we settled on five elements upon which great practice rests.

PILLAR #1: AN EXCELLENT TEACHER OR COACH

One of my core beliefs is that everything rises and falls on leadership. I teach that truth to businesspeople all the time, but it also applies in other areas of life, including practice. People who perform at their peak practice effectively, and they practice effectively under the leadership of a great teacher.

Howard Hendricks, professor and chairman of the Center for Christian Leadership in Dallas, says, "Teaching is causing people to learn." How do good coaches do that? In part, they inspire. But good teachers do more than that. They tailor their instruction to their students. A good teacher or coach, like all good leaders, knows the strengths and weaknesses of each person. He knows whether a person is a right-brain creative/intuitive type or a left-brain analytical type. He knows whether a person learns visually, verbally, or kinesthetically. And he can tell when someone needs a pat on the back or a kick in the pants.

PILLAR #2: YOUR BEST EFFORT

Industrialist and philanthropist Andrew Carnegie declared, "There is no use whatever trying to help people who do not help themselves. You cannot push anyone up a ladder unless he is willing to climb himself." People don't improve and reach their potential without putting forth great effort. That's why composer and orchestra leader Duke Ellington used to make a simple but demanding request of the musicians who played for him. "Just give me your best," he asked. Ellington worked hard and expected the same from others, knowing that hard work would not kill anybody (although it does seem to scare some people half to death).

Joe Theismann, who was a longtime announcer for ESPN, quarterbacked the Washington Redskins to two Super Bowl appearances in 1983 and 1984. The team won the first time and lost the second time. Today he wears his Super Bowl winner's ring and his "loser's" ring as reminders of the importance of effort. Why? Because his two experiences couldn't have been more different. During their championship season,

Theismann was thrilled to be in the Super Bowl and gave his very best to win. But not the next year. About the next year, Theismann explained, "I was griping about the weather, my shoes, practice times, everything." He clearly wasn't giving his best effort. "The difference in those two rings," said Theismann, "lies in applying oneself and not accepting anything but the best."[1]

PILLAR #3: A CLEAR PURPOSE

PGA golfer Warren Bottke says that when he works with a new client, the first thing he does is to establish the purpose of practice. That usually means identifying a specific goal for each practice session. But the overarching purpose of practice is always improvement leading to excellence.

Pepperdine University sociology professor Jon Johnston makes a distinction between excellence and mere success:

> Success bases our worth on a comparison with others. Excellence gauges our value by measuring us against our own potential. Success grants its rewards to the few but is the dream of the multitudes. Excellence is available to all living beings but is accepted by the . . . few. Success focuses its attention on the external—becoming the tastemaker for the insatiable appetites of the . . . consumer. Excellence beams its spotlight on the internal spirit . . . Excellence cultivates principles and consistency.[2]

As you practice, make excellence your target, and give your best to achieve it. If excellence is your goal and you arrive at it, you will be satisfied even though you never achieve success.

Pillar #4: The Greatest Potential

Have you ever noticed that two people on the same team with the same coach can practice with equal focus, effort, and purpose and have very different results? It's a fact that equal practice does not mean equal progress. I learned this fact when I was nine. By then I had been taking piano lessons for a couple of years. As I played, I thought to myself, *I'm pretty good at this.* But then one day I played at a piano recital, and it turned out to be a reality check. Elaine, a girl who had been taking piano lessons for only six months, played a more difficult piece than mine. How could she be so much better than I was so quickly? The answer was simple: her potential was much greater than mine. It didn't matter how much focused effort I put into practicing the piano. I was never going to go as far as Elaine could. Music wasn't one of my best gifts. I enjoyed playing, but I wasn't going to achieve excellence in it.

A few years ago after I spoke on leadership for Chick-fil-A, someone asked me during a Q and A session how to develop future leaders. I believe that when I quickly answered, "Find potential leaders," people thought I was being flippant. But my point was that it's much easier to train people in the area of their greatest potential. When I evaluate people's potential, I ask two questions: (1) Can they? and (2) Will they? The answers to these questions reveal something about their ability and their attitude. If both are right, the potential for excellence is high.

Once you figure out where your greatest potential lies, then start to practice there. If you don't, not only will you fail to increase your ability, but you'll eventually lose some of the ability you started with. You see, having potential works exactly opposite from the way a savings account does. When you put your money in a savings account, as time goes by, your money compounds and grows. The longer you leave it untouched, the more it *increases*. But when it comes to potential, the longer you leave it untouched, the more it *decreases*. If you don't tap into your talent, it wastes away.

One way you can get the best from yourself is to set high standards for your greatest potential. Dianne Snedaker, former cofounder and general partner of Wingspring, advises,

> If you are interested in success, it's easy to set your standards in terms of other people's accomplishments and then let other people measure you by those standards. But the standards you set for yourself are always more important. They should be higher than the standards anyone else would set for you, because in the end you have to live with yourself, and judge yourself, and feel good about yourself. And the best way to do that is to live up to your highest potential. So set your standards high and keep them high, even if you think no one else is looking. Somebody out there will always notice, even if it's just you.

You can tell that you're not making the most of your potential when the standards set for you by others are higher than the ones you set for yourself. Anytime you require less of yourself than your boss, spouse, coach, or other involved person does, your potential will go untapped.

PILLAR #5: THE RIGHT RESOURCES

Even if you do many things right, including finding a good coach or mentor, focusing in your area of greatest potential, giving your best, and doing so with purpose, you can still fall short without the right resources. During World War II, General George Patton was one of the most talented and accomplished commanders for the Allied forces. He was innovative, focused, and fearless. He was a good strategist and tactician. And he possessed the tanks and men to strike boldly against the Nazis to help bring an end to the war. But one thing he often lacked: gasoline. Without fuel, his tanks were useless.

Resources are nothing more than tools you need to accomplish your purpose. Every human endeavor requires resources of some kind. To practice well, you need to be properly equipped.

THE EXTRA THAT MAKES PEOPLE SUCCESSFUL

There is one more secret to successful practice that will help you sharpen your talent, and I believe it elevates top achievers above everyone else. It's summed up by the phrase "a little extra." Here's what I believe it takes for someone to become successful in the area of practice:

1. A LITTLE EXTRA EFFORT

Historian Charles Kendall Adams, who was president of Cornell University and later the University of Wisconsin, observed, "No one ever attains very eminent success by simply doing what is required of him; it is the amount of excellence of what is over and above the required that determines greatness." All accomplishments begin with the willingness to try—and then some. The difference between the ordinary and the extraordinary is the *extra*!

A little extra effort always gives a person an edge. Art Williams, the founder of Primerica Financial Services, once told me, "You beat fifty percent of the people in America by working hard; you beat forty percent by being a person of honesty and integrity and standing for something; and the last ten percent is a dogfight in the free enterprise system." If you want to win that dogfight, then do a little extra.

2. A LITTLE EXTRA TIME

Successful people practice harder and practice longer than unsuccessful people do. Success expert Peter Lowe, who has gleaned success secrets from hundreds of people who are at the top of their profession, says, "The most common trait I have found in all successful people is that they have conquered the temptation to give up."

Giving a little extra time requires more than just perseverance. It requires patience. The Law of Process in my book *The 21 Irrefutable Laws of Leadership* says, "Leadership develops daily, not in a day." That can be said of any talent we try to cultivate and improve.

As you work to give a little extra time to your efforts, it is wise to maintain a longer view of the process of improvement. Such a perspective really helps. Gutzon Borglum, the sculptor who created the memorial to the American presidents at Mount Rushmore, was asked if he considered his work to be perfect. It's said he replied, "Not today. The nose of Washington is an inch too long. It's better that way, though. It will erode to be exactly right in ten thousand years." Now that's patience!

3. A Little Extra Help

Anybody who succeeds at anything does so with the help of others. Alex Haley, the author of *Roots*, used to keep a reminder of that in his office. It said, "If you see a turtle on top of a fence post, you know he had help getting there."

I know that in my professional pursuits, I've always needed help. And I've been fortunate that others were willing to give it to me. Early in my career in the 1970s, I contacted the top ten leaders in my field and offered them one hundred dollars to meet with me for thirty minutes so that I could ask them questions. Many granted my request, and (fortunately for my thin wallet at the time) most declined to accept the hundred dollars. And today I still make it a point to meet with excellent leaders from whom I desire to learn.

When I think about the ways people have helped me in all aspects of my life, I am humbled and grateful. Some have given me advice. Others have presented me with opportunities. And a few, like my wife, Margaret, have lavished unconditional love on me. I know I am a very fortunate man.

4. A Little Extra Change

A letter was returned to the post office. Handwritten on the envelope were the words, "He's dead." Through an oversight, the letter was inadvertently sent again to the same address. It was again returned to the post office with another handwritten message: "He's still dead!"

Let's face it. Most people are resistant to change. They desire improvement, but they resist changing their everyday routine. That's a problem because, as leadership expert Max DePree says, "We cannot become what we need to be by remaining what we are." To sharpen your talent through practice, you need to do more than just be *open* to change. You need to *pursue* change—and you need to do it a little bit more than other achievers. Here's what to look for and how to focus your energy to get the kinds of changes that will change you for the better:

- Don't change just enough to *get away* from your problems—change enough to *solve* them.
- Don't change your *circumstances* to improve your life— change *yourself* to improve your circumstances.
- Don't do *the same old things* expecting to get different results—get different results by doing *something new*.
- Don't wait to *see the light* to change—start changing as soon as you *feel the heat*.
- Don't see change as something *hurtful* that *must* be done—see it as something *helpful* that *can* be done.
- Don't avoid paying the *immediate* price of change—if you do, you will pay the *ultimate* price of never improving.

Poet and philosopher Johann von Schiller wrote, "He who has done his best for his own time has lived for all times." You can do your best only if you are continually seeking to embrace positive change.

When you have worked hard in practice to sharpen your talent and you begin to see results, please don't think that it's time to stop practicing. You never arrive at your potential— you can only continue to strive toward it. And that means continual practice.

Charles Swindoll's friend William Johnson, who owned the Ritz-Carlton hotels, was pleased when the organization won the Malcolm Baldridge National Quality Award. When Swindoll congratulated him, Johnson quickly gave others the credit for the achievement. But he also said that it made him and others in the organization work even harder to earn the respect that came with the award. Johnson summed up his attitude: "Quality is a race with no finish line." If you don't strive for excellence, then you are soon settling for acceptable. The next step is mediocrity, and nobody pays for mediocre! If you want to reach your potential and be more successful, you have to keep practicing with excellence.

Chapter 8

Embody Perseverance

Perseverance is not an issue of talent. It is not an issue of time. It is about finishing. Talent provides hope for accomplishment, but perseverance guarantees it. Playwright Noel Coward commented, "Thousands of people have talent. I might as well congratulate you for having eyes in your head. The one and only thing that counts is: Do you have staying power?"

PRINCIPLES OF PERSEVERANCE

No matter how talented people are, there is no success without perseverance. World War I flying ace Eddie Rickenbacker said, "I can give you a six-word formula for success: Think things through—then follow through." Many people like to think things through; few follow through.

If you desire to become successful, you need to understand some things about perseverance:

1. Perseverance Means Succeeding Because You Are Determined To, Not Destined To

Green Bay Packers coach Vince Lombardi said, "The difference between a successful person and others is not lack of strength, not a lack of knowledge, but rather a lack of determination." The greatest achievers don't sit back and wait for success because they think they deserve it. They keep moving forward and persevering because they are determined to achieve it.

You can see this determination in successful people in every walk of life and in every age. Hannibal, the Carthaginian general who fought the Romans during the Second Punic War, asserted, "We will either find a way or make one." He lived out that attitude of perseverance when he led an unexpected campaign that took him over the Alps to defeat the Romans.

Joseph Lanier, one-time chairman and CEO of West Point-Pepperell, Inc., stated, "We are determined to win the battle. We will fight them until hell freezes over, and then, if we have to, we'll fight them on the ice." That kind of determination serves people well whether they are running an organization or pursuing a profession.

2. Perseverance Recognizes Life Is Not a Long Race but Many Short Ones in Succession

Have you heard the saying, "Life is a marathon"? Whoever first said it was almost certainly trying to encourage people to keep trying when things get tough and to have a patient yet tenacious approach to life. But I think whoever said it didn't quite get it right. Life isn't one very long race. It's actually a long series of shorter races, one after another. Each task has its own challenges. Each day is its own event. True, you have to get out of bed the next day and race again, but it's never exactly the same race as before. To be successful, you just need to keep plugging away. Talk show host Rush Limbaugh observed, "In life or in football, touchdowns rarely take place in seventy-yard increments. Usually it's three yards and a cloud of dust."

I've read that explorer Christopher Columbus faced incredible difficulties while sailing west in search of a passage to Asia. He and his crews encountered storms, experienced hunger and deprivation, and dealt with extreme discouragement. The crews of the three ships were near mutiny. But Columbus persevered. The account of the journey written by Columbus said the same thing, day after day: "Today we sailed on." And his perseverance paid off. He didn't discover a fast route to the spice-rich Indies; instead he found new continents. But as he sailed, his focus was clear—making it through the day. Winning each short race. And that's key. Management consultant Laddie F. Hutar affirmed that "success consists of a series of little daily victories."

3. Perseverance Is Needed to Release Most of Life's Rewards

At a sales convention, the corporate sales manager got up in front of all two thousand of his firm's salespeople and asked, "Did the Wright brothers ever quit?"

"No!" the sales force shouted.

"Did Charles Lindbergh ever quit?" he asked.

"No!" the salespeople shouted again.

"Did Lance Armstrong ever quit?"

"No!"

He bellowed for a fourth time, "Did Thorndike McKester ever quit?" There was a confused silence for a long moment.

Then a salesperson stood up and asked, "Who in the world is Thorndike McKester? Nobody's ever heard of him."

The sales manager snapped back, "Of course you never heard of him—because he quit!"[1]

How many highly successful people do you know who gave up? How many do you know who have been richly rewarded for quitting? I don't know any, and I bet you don't either. It's said that Walt Disney's request for a loan was rejected by more than three hundred banks before he finally got a yes. The loan he received allowed him to build Disneyland, the first and most famous theme park in history.

Inventor Thomas Edison asserted, "Many of life's failures are people who did not realize how close they were to success when they gave up." It's the last step in the race that counts the most. That is where the winner is determined. That is where the rewards come. If you run every step of the race well *except* the last one and you stop before the finish line, then the end result will be the same as if you never ran a step.

4. PERSEVERANCE DRAWS SWEETNESS OUT OF ADVERSITY

The trials and pressures of life—and how we face them—often define us. Confronted by adversity, many people give up while others rise up. How do those who succeed do it? They persevere. They find the benefit to them personally that comes from any trial. And they recognize that the best thing about adversity is coming out on the other side of it. There is a sweetness to overcoming your troubles and finding something good in the process, however small it may be.

I came across a poem by Howard Goodman called "I Don't Regret a Mile" that expresses this idea well. It says, in part:

I've dreamed many a dream that's never come true,
I've seen them vanish at dawn,
But enough of my dreams have come true
To make me keep dreaming on
I've prayed many a prayer that seemed no answer
     would come,
Though I'd waited so patient and long;
But enough answers have come to my prayers
To make me keep praying on
I've sown many a seed that's fallen by the wayside,
For the birds to feed upon
But I've held enough golden sheaves in my hands
To make me keep sowing on
I've trusted many a friend that's failed me
And left me to weep alone
But enough of my friends have been true-blue
To make me keep trusting on
I've drained the cup of disappointment and pain,
And gone many a day without song
But I've sipped enough nectar from the roses of life
To make me want to live on.[2]

Giving up when adversity threatens can make a person bitter. Persevering through adversity makes one better.

5. Perseverance Has a Compounding Effect on Life

Author Napoleon Hill says, "Every successful person finds that great success lies just beyond the point when they're convinced their idea is not going to work." How do you get beyond that point? How do you go beyond what you believe is your limit? How do you achieve *lasting* success? Do the right thing, day after day. There are no shortcuts to anything worthwhile.

Every day that you do the right things—work hard, treat others with respect, learn, and grow—you invest in yourself. To do these things every day takes relentless perseverance, but if you do them, your success compounds over time. Weight-loss expert and author Judy Wardell Halliday supported this idea: "Dreams become reality when we keep our commitment to them."

6. Perseverance Means Stopping Not Because You're Tired but Because the Task Is Done

Former diplomat and recipient of the Presidential Medal of Freedom Robert Strauss commented, "Success is a little like wrestling a gorilla. You don't quit when you're tired—you quit when the gorilla is tired." If you think about it, perseverance doesn't really come into play until you *are* tired. When you're fresh, excited, and energetic, you approach a task with vigor. Work is fun. Only when you become tired do you need perseverance.

To successful people, fatigue and discouragement are not signs to quit. They perceive them as signals to draw on their reserves, rely on their character, and keep going. One problem of many people is that they underestimate what it will take to succeed. Enlightenment political philosopher Montesquieu declared, "In most things success depends on knowing how long it takes to succeed." When we haven't counted the cost of success, we approach challenges with mere interest; what is really required is total commitment. And that makes all the difference.

7. PERSEVERANCE DOESN'T DEMAND MORE THAN WE HAVE BUT ALL THAT WE HAVE

Author Frank Tyger observed, "In every triumph there is a lot of try." But perseverance means more than trying. It means more than working hard. Perseverance is an investment. It is a willingness to bind oneself emotionally, intellectually, physically, and spiritually to an idea or task until it has been completed. Perseverance demands a lot, but here's the good news: everything you give is an investment in yourself.

THE FIVE ENEMIES OF PERSEVERANCE

French scientist Louis Pasteur said, "Let me tell you the secret that has led me to my goal. My strength lives solely in my tenacity." Perseverance begins with the right attitude—an attitude of tenacity. But the desire to persevere alone isn't enough to keep most people going when they are tired or discouraged. Perseverance is a trait that can be cultivated. And the initial step to developing it is to eliminate its five greatest enemies:

1. A LIFESTYLE OF GIVING UP

A little boy had been promised an ice-cream cone if he was good while accompanying his grandfather on some errands. The longer they were gone, the more difficult the boy was finding it to be good. "How much longer will it be?" the boy asked.

"Not too long," replied the grandfather. "We've got just one more stop before we get ice cream."

"I don't know if I can make it, Grandpa," the little boy

responded. "I can be good. I just can't be good enough long enough."

When we were kids and we didn't follow through on a task, people often gave us a break. That's to be expected. Children tend to jump from one activity to another and to bounce from idea to idea. Adults can't do that and expect to be successful. Scientist L. G. Elliott advised, "Vacillating people seldom succeed. They seldom win the solid respect of their fellows. Successful men and women are very careful in reaching decisions and very persistent and determined in action thereafter."

If you desire to be successful and to maximize your talent, you need to be consistent and persistent. Talent without perseverance never comes to full fruition. Opportunities without persistence will be lost. There is a direct correlation between perseverance and potential. If you have a habit of giving up, you need to overcome it to be successful.

2. A Wrong Belief That Life Should Be Easy

Debra K. Johnson tells about an incident with her seven-year-old daughter who wanted to take violin lessons. When they went to a music store together to rent an instrument, Debra began lecturing her about the expense of lessons and the commitment that would be required of her if she got her the violin. "There will be times you'll feel like giving up," Debra said, "but I want you to hang in there and keep on trying."

Her daughter nodded and, in her most serious voice, responded, "It will be just like marriage, right, Mom?" Having the right expectations going into anything is half the battle.

John C. Norcross, a clinical psychologist and professor at

the University of Scranton, has studied people and their goals, and he has found a characteristic that distinguishes those who reach their goals from those who don't: expectations. Both types of people experience the same amount of failure during the first month they strive for their goals. But members of the successful group don't expect to succeed right away, and they view their failures as a reason to recommit and a reminder to refocus on their goals with more determination. Norcross says, "Those who are unsuccessful say a relapse is evidence that they can't do it."[3]

3. A Wrong Belief That Success Is a Destination

The NBA's Pat Riley has won many championships as a basketball coach. In his book *The Winner Within*, he wrote, "Complacency is the last hurdle any winner, any team must overcome before attaining potential greatness. Complacency is the success disease: it takes root when you're feeling good about who you are and what you've achieved."[4] It's ironic, but past success can be the fiercest enemy to future success.

If you think you have arrived, then you're in trouble. As soon as you think you no longer need to work to make progress, you'll begin to lose ground.

4. A Lack of Resiliency

Harvard professor of psychiatry George E. Vaillant, in his book *Aging Well*, identifies resiliency as a significant characteristic of people who navigate the many transitions of life from birth to old age. He wrote, "Resilience reflects individuals who metaphorically resemble a twig with a fresh, green living core. When twisted out of shape, such a twig bends, but it does not break; instead it springs back and continues growing."[5]

That's an excellent description of how we must be if we desire to persevere through adversity and make the most of the talent we have. We must not become dry, brittle, and inflexible. And we must endeavor to bounce back, no matter how we may feel. We would be wise to remember the words of former NBA player, coach, and executive Jerry West: "You can't get much done in life if you only work on the days you feel good."

5. A Lack of Vision

Everything that is created is actually created twice. First it is created mentally; then it is created physically. Where does that mental creation come from? The answer is vision.

People who display perseverance keep a larger vision in mind as they toil away at their craft or profession. They see in their mind's eye what they want to create or to do, and they keep working toward it as they labor. For example, years ago I read an account of an amateur golfer who played a round with Sam Snead, member of the World Golf Hall of Fame, recipient of the PGA Tour Lifetime Achievement Award, and three-time captain of the U.S. Ryder Cup team. On the first hole, Snead shot a seven—three over par, an unusually poor score for a golfer of his caliber. As the pair exited the green, Snead didn't seem to be bothered by his triple bogey. When his amateur companion asked Snead about it, he responded, "That's why we play eighteen holes." Snead's vision of the big picture helped him maintain perspective, remain resilient, and persevere. By the end of the round, Snead finished four strokes under par.

HOW TO MULTIPLY YOUR PERSEVERANCE

Clearing away the five enemies of perseverance is a preliminary step to becoming successful in the area of perseverance. Right thinking always precedes right action. If you want to be able to sustain your talent, then take the following steps:

PURPOSE: FIND ONE

Rich De Voss, owner of the NBA's Orlando Magic, remarked, "Persistence is stubbornness with a purpose." It is very difficult for people to develop perseverance when they lack a sense of purpose. Conversely, when one has a passionate sense of purpose, energy rises, obstacles become incidental, and perseverance wins out.

Perhaps you've seen *America's Most Wanted*, the television program that recreates the crime stories and encourages viewers to help authorities locate and capture the criminals who are wanted for these often violent crimes. The program's host is John Walsh. Many people think he is an actor or a journalist—a television professional hired to host the show. But he isn't, and his story is quite remarkable.

Walsh owned his own company, and along with three partners, he built deluxe hotels. But one day his six-year-old son, Adam, disappeared. The child had been abducted, but because there was no evidence of a crime, the authorities were slow to help Walsh and his wife find their only child. They searched for sixteen days. Tragically, by the time he was found, it was too late. He was dead.

Walsh's life was thrown into chaos. He lost thirty pounds. His house went into foreclosure. And he lost his business—he just couldn't bring himself to return to his work. He had lost all hope. Then one day Dr. Ronald Wright, the county coroner, looked at Walsh and asked, "You're thinking about suicide, aren't you?"

"What do I have to live for?" Walsh replied. "I have nothing. My only child has been murdered. I can't even talk to my wife. I have no job, my house is in foreclosure, my whole life is over."

"No, it isn't," Wright responded. "You are articulate. You mounted the greatest campaign for a missing child in the history of Florida. Go out and try to change things."

Walsh says that it was the best advice he'd gotten from anyone. It gave him purpose. And that sense of purpose did more than give him a reason not to kill himself. It energized him to serve and help others. In 1988, he began hosting *America's Most Wanted*. The show ultimately was responsible for the capture of hundreds of fugitives, including fourteen who were on the FBI's Ten Most Wanted lists.

If you want to be successful, you need to find your purpose. That is the only way you will be able to persevere, as John Walsh did, even when facing the most difficult circumstances.

EXCUSES: ELIMINATE THEM

One of the most striking things that separates people who sustain their success from those who are only briefly or never successful is their strong sense of responsibility for their own actions. It is easier to move from failure to success than it is from excuses to success.

According to Bruce Nash, author of a series of "Hall of Shame" books on sports figures, one notorious person for making excuses was Rafael Septien, former placekicker for the

NFL's Dallas Cowboys. Nash wrote, "We're all guilty of using excuses. When we do, we place ourselves in the company of great sports heroes. Take Rafael Septien, for example. Rafael Septien has no peers—when it comes to making up lame-brained excuses for missed field goals." Among the excuses, perhaps tongue-in-cheek, that Septien offered:

- "I was too busy reading my stats on the scoreboard."
- "The grass was too tall." (Texas Stadium doesn't even have grass; its surface is artificial turf.)
- "The thirty-second clock distracted me."
- "My helmet was too tight and it was squeezing my brain. I couldn't think."
- "No wonder [I missed]. You placed the ball upside down" (said to his holder).[6]

If you want to maximize and sustain your talent, don't allow yourself to offer excuses when you don't perform at the best of your ability. Instead, take complete responsibility for yourself and your actions. And keep in mind the words of George Washington Carver, who said, "Ninety-nine percent of failures come from people who have the habit of making excuses."

STAMINA: DEVELOP SOME

Former world heavyweight champion boxer Muhammad Ali, called "The Greatest," asserted, "Champions aren't made in the gyms. Champions are made from something they have deep inside them—a desire, a dream, a vision. They have to have last-minute stamina, they have to be a little faster, they have to have the skill, and the will. But the will must be stronger than the skill." All people who achieve and maintain success possess stamina. Truly, stamina is a key to perseverance, and perseverance is a key to becoming successful.

Earlier in this chapter I stated that life is not one long race but a series of many short ones in succession. That's true no matter what your talent is or what skills you possess. Without perseverance, a talented person is little more than a flash in the pan. With perseverance, a person has a solid chance to be successful.

CHAPTER 9

DEMONSTRATE COURAGE

People think of courage as a quality required only in times of extreme danger or stress, such as during war or disaster. But it is much larger than that—and more ordinary than we think. Courage is an everyday virtue. Professor, writer, and apologist C. S. Lewis wrote, "Courage is not simply one of the virtues, but the form of every virtue at its testing point."[1] You can do nothing worthwhile without courage. The person who exhibits courage is often able to live without regrets.

WHY DOES TALENT NEED COURAGE?

English writer and clergyman Sydney Smith asserted, "A great deal of talent is lost to the world for want of a little courage." To develop and discover our talent, we need courage. The English word *courage* comes from the French word *coeur*, which means "heart." And we need to recognize that if we display courage, our hearts will be tested continually. Here's what I mean:

Our Courage Will Be Tested . . . as We Seek a Truth That We Know May Be Painful

All of us will be tested in life. Often those tests are private and involve an internal battle, and many people find that painful. These tests require us to look at ourselves honestly. Pulitzer Prize–winning columnist Herbert Agar said, "The truth that makes men free is for the most part the truth which men prefer not to hear."

In order to grow, we need to face truths about ourselves, and that is often a difficult process. It usually looks something like this:

- **The issue.** Often it is something we do not want to hear about.
- **The temptation.** We want to ignore it, rationalize it, spin it, or package it.
- **The decision.** To grow, we must face the truth and make personal changes.
- **The challenge.** Change is not easy; our decision to change will be tested daily.
- **The response.** Others will be slow to acknowledge it; they will wait to see if our behavior changes.
- **The respect.** Respect is always gained on difficult ground, and it comes from others only when our behavior and words match.

Winston Churchill, the great statesman and British prime minister during World War II, said, "Courage is what it takes to stand up and speak; courage is also what it takes to sit down and listen." It takes a brave person to listen to unpleasant truths. I have to admit that this has been a challenging area for me. I find it much easier to cast vision, motivate people, and lead the charge than to sit, listen to others speak truth, humble myself, and respond appropriately, but I'm continuing to work on it.

Our Courage Will Be Tested . . . When Change Is Needed but Inactivity Is More Comfortable

Being inactive and never leaving what is familiar may mean that you are comfortable, but having the willingness to continually let go of the familiar means that you are courageous. American historian James Harvey Robinson asserted, "Greatness, in the last analysis, is largely due to bravery—courage in escaping from old ideas and old standards and respectable ways of doing things."

Our situation doesn't make us; we make our situation. Our circumstances don't have to define us; we can redefine our circumstances by our actions. At any given time, we must be willing to give up all we have in order to become all we can be. If we do that, if we are willing to leave our comfort zone and bravely keep striving, we can reach heights we thought were beyond us. We can go further than others who possess greater talent than we do. Italian actress Sophia Loren observed, "Getting ahead in a difficult profession requires avid faith in yourself. That is why some people with mediocre talent, but with the inner drive, go much farther than people with vastly superior talent."

Our Courage Will Be Tested . . . When Our Convictions, Once Expressed, Are Challenged

Anytime you are willing to stand up for something, someone else will be willing to take a shot at you. People who express their convictions and attempt to live them out will experience conflict from others with opposing views. Ralph Waldo Emerson wrote, "Whatever you do, you need courage. Whatever course you decide upon, there is always someone to tell you you are wrong. There are always difficulties arising which tempt you to believe that your critics are right. To map out a course of action and follow it to an end, requires some of the same courage which a soldier needs. Peace has its victories, but it takes brave men to win them."[2] So should we simply keep a low profile, swallow our convictions, and keep the peace? Of course not! The opposite of courage isn't cowardice; it is conformity. It's not enough just to believe in something. We need to live for something. Howard Hendricks said, "A belief is something you will argue about. A conviction is something you will die for." You cannot really live unless there are things in your life for which you are willing to die.

OUR COURAGE WILL BE TESTED . . . WHEN LEARNING AND GROWING WILL DISPLAY OUR WEAKNESS

Learning and growing always require action, and action takes courage—especially in the weak areas of our lives. That is where fear most often comes into play. It's easy to be brave in an area of strength; it's much more difficult in an area of weakness. That is why we need courage most. General Omar Bradley remarked, "Bravery is the capacity to perform properly even when scared half to death."

When I am striving to learn and grow in an area of weakness and I am afraid of failing or looking foolish, I encourage myself with these quotations:

- "Courage is fear holding on a minute longer."—George S. Patton
- "The difference between a hero and a coward is one step sideways."—Gene Hackman
- "Courage is fear that has said its prayers."—Karl Barth
- "Courage is doing what you're afraid to do. There can be no courage unless you're scared."—Eddie Rickenbacker
- "Courage is being scared to death but saddling up anyway."—John Wayne

David Ben-Gurion, the first prime minister of Israel, observed, "Courage is a special kind of knowledge; the knowledge of how to fear what ought to be feared, and how not to fear what ought not to be feared. From this knowledge comes an inner strength that subconsciously inspires us to push on in the face of great difficulty. What can seem impossible is often possible, with courage." Courage is a releasing force for learning and growth.

OUR COURAGE WILL BE TESTED . . . WHEN WE TAKE THE HIGH ROAD EVEN AS OTHERS TREAT US BADLY

In 2004, I wrote a book called *Winning with People: Discover the People Principles That Work for You Every Time*. In it is the High Road Principle, which says, "We go to a higher level when we treat others better than they treat us." When it comes to dealing with others, there are really only three routes we can take:

The low road—where we treat others worse than they treat us

The middle road—where we treat others the same as they
   treat us
The high road—where we treat others better than they
   treat us[3]

The low road damages relationships and alienates others
from us. The middle road may not drive people away, but it
doesn't attract them either. But the high road creates positive
relationships with others and attracts people to us—even in
the midst of conflict.

Taking the high road requires two things. The first is
courage. It certainly isn't one's immediate inclination to turn
the other cheek and treat people well while they treat you
badly. How does one find the courage to do that? By relying
on the second thing, about which clergyman Dr. James B.
Mooneyhan wrote:

> There is a great cancer working at the integrity of our society.
> It gets in the way of our efficiency and hampers our success. It
> robs us of the promotions we seek and the prestige we desire.
> The great tragedy is that none of us are immune to it automat-
> ically. Each of us must work to overcome it.

This malignancy is the lack of the ability to forgive. When
someone wrongs us we make mental notes to remember what
was done or we think of ways to "get back at them." Someone
gets the promotion we wanted so badly and resentment toward
that person begins to build. Our spouse makes a mistake or
does something offensive to us and we see what we can do to
get even or at least make sure they never forget the hurt they
have caused us.

When we keep score of wrongs committed against us, we reveal a lack of maturity. Theodore Roosevelt once said, "The most important single ingredient in the formula of success is knowing how to get along with people." Those who do not forgive are persons who have not yet learned this truth and they are usually unsuccessful people.

If you wish to improve this area of your life, here are some things that should help.

First, practice forgiving.

Second, think good thoughts of those persons. It is difficult to have hostile feelings toward one in whom you see good.

Finally, let people know through your actions that you are one who can forgive and forget. This will gain respect for you.

Remember this: committing an injury puts you below your enemy; taking revenge only makes you even with him, but forgiving him sets you above.

No one makes the most of his talent in isolation. Becoming your best will require the participation of other people. When you take the high road with others, you make yourself the kind of person others want to work with—and you put yourself in the best position to help others at the same time.

Our Courage Will Be Tested . . . When Being "Out Front" Makes Us an Easy Target

Many people admire leaders and innovators. Organizations give them honors; historians write books about them; sculptors chisel their images on the face of mountains. However, while many people lift leaders up, others want to knock them down. C. V. White describes this tension well:

> The man who makes a success of an important venture never waits for the crowd. He strikes out for himself. It takes nerve, it takes a lot of grit; but the man that succeeds has both. Anyone can fail. The public admires the man who has enough confidence in himself to take the chance. These chances are the main things after all. The man who tries to succeed must expect to be criticized. Nothing important was ever done but the greater number consulted previously doubted the possibility. Success is the accomplishment of that which people think can't be done.[4]

If you are a leader or even an innovative thinker, you will often be ahead of the crowd, and that will at times make you an easy target. That requires courage.

For many years, I hosted an event in Atlanta called Exchange. It was a weekend leadership experience for executives. I usually did some leadership teaching, brought in some high-profile leaders to answer questions, and arranged a unique leadership experience. One year we took the group to the King Center so that they could be impacted by the life and legacy of a great leader, Martin Luther King Jr. We then took them over to Ebenezer Baptist Church. And as a surprise we had arranged for King's widow, Coretta Scott King, and daughter Bernice to be there so that everyone could meet them.

One question asked of Mrs. King was what it was like being with Dr. King during the civil rights movement, and she talked about the loneliness of being a pioneer and taking new territory. She said that her husband was often misunderstood, and she pointed out how much courage it took to stand alone.

We will almost certainly never have to face the hatred and violence that Martin Luther King Jr. did, but that doesn't mean that we don't need courage to lead. Often leaders are misunderstood, their motives are misconstrued, and their actions are criticized. That, too, can be a test—one that makes us stronger and sharpens our talent if only we have the courage to endure it.

Our Courage Will Be Tested . . . Whenever We Face Obstacles to Our Progress

Advice columnist Ann Landers wrote, "If I were asked to give what I consider the single most useful bit of advice for all humanity, it would be this: Expect trouble as an inevitable part of life and when it comes, hold your head high, look it squarely in the eye and say, 'I will be bigger than you. You cannot defeat me.'"

Adversity is always the partner of progress. Anytime we want to move forward, obstacles, difficulties, problems, and predicaments are going to get in the way. We should expect nothing less. And we should even welcome such things. Novelist H. G. Wells asked, "What on earth would a man do with himself if something didn't stand in his way?" Why would he make such a comment? Because he recognized that adversity is our friend, even though it doesn't feel that way. Every obstacle we overcome teaches us about ourselves, about our strengths and weaknesses. Every obstacle shapes us. When we succeed in the midst of difficulty, we become stronger, wiser, and more confident. The greatest people in history are those who faced the most difficult challenges with courage and rose to the occasion.

Pat Williams, in his book *American Scandal*, wrote about Churchill's last months. He says in 1964, former president and World War II general Dwight D. Eisenhower went to visit the former prime minister. Eisenhower sat by the bold-spirited leader's bed for a long period of time, neither speaking. After about ten minutes, Churchill slowly raised his hand and painstakingly made the "V" for victory sign, which he had so often flashed to the British public during the war. Eisenhower, fighting back tears, pulled his chair back, stood up, saluted him, and left the room. To his aide out in the hallway, Eisenhower said, "I just said goodbye to Winston, but you never say farewell to courage."[5]

WHERE TO FIND COURAGE

It's tempting to learn about the life of someone like Churchill or Eisenhower and believe that certain people are born with courage and are destined for greatness while others must sit on the sidelines and simply admire them. But I don't think that is true. I believe anyone can develop courage. If you desire to become a more courageous person, then do the following:

1. LOOK FOR COURAGE INSIDE, NOT OUTSIDE, OF YOURSELF

During the Great Depression, Thomas Edison delivered his last public message. In it he said, "My message to you is: Be courageous! I have lived a long time. I have seen history repeat itself again and again. I have seen many depressions in business. Always America has come out stronger and more prosperous. Be as brave as your fathers before you. Have faith! Go forward!"[6] Edison knew that when we experience fear, we must be willing to move forward. That is an individual decision. Courage starts internally before it is displayed externally. We must first win the battle within ourselves.

The old saying goes, "If we could kick the person responsible for most of our troubles, we wouldn't be able to sit down for a week." Courage, like all other character qualities, comes from within. It begins as a decision we make and grows as we make the choice to follow through.

2. Grow in Courage by Doing the Right Thing Instead of the Expedient Thing

Florence Nightingale observed, "Courage is . . . the universal virtue of all those who choose to do the right thing over the expedient thing. It is the common currency of all those who do what they are supposed to do in a time of conflict, crisis, and confusion." The acquisition of courage can often be an internal battle. We often desire to do what is most expedient. The problem is that what is easy and expedient is frequently not what is right. Thus the battle. But psychotherapist and author Sheldon Kopp stated, "All the significant battles are waged within self."

As you strive to do what you know to be right, you must know yourself and make sure you are acting in integrity with your core values. There's a saying that inside every individual there are six people. They are . . .

Who You Are Reputed to Be
Who You Are Expected to Be

Who You Were
Who You Wish to Be
Who You Think You Are
Who You Really Are

You must strive to be true to who you really are. If you do and you do the right thing, then you will increase in courage.

3. Take Small Steps of Courage to Prepare You for Greater Ones

Most of us want to grow quickly and be done with it. The reality is that genuine growth is slow, and to be successful, we should start with small things and do them every day. St. Francis de Sales advised, "Have patience with all things, but chiefly have patience with yourself. Do not lose courage in considering your own imperfections, but instantly start remedying them—every day begin the task anew."

People's lives change when they change something they do every day. That's how they change the "who they wish to be" into "who they really are." What kinds of things can you do every day? You can have the courage to be positive as you get up in the morning to face the day. You can have the courage to be gracious in defeat. You can have the courage to apologize when you hurt someone or make a mistake. You can have the courage to try something new—any small thing. Each time you display bravery of any kind, you make an investment in your courage. Do that long enough, and you will begin to live a *lifestyle* of courage. And when the bigger risks come, they will seem much smaller to you because you will have become much larger.

You just need to want to reach your potential and to be willing to trade what seems good in the moment for what's best for your potential. That's something you can do regardless of your level of natural talent.

CHAPTER 10

BECOME MORE TEACHABLE

If you are a highly talented person, you may have a tough time with teachability. Why? Because talented people often think they know it all. And that makes it difficult for them to continually expand their talent. Teachability is not so much about competence and mental capacity as it is about *attitude*. It is the desire to listen, learn, and apply. It is the hunger to discover and grow. It is the willingness to learn, unlearn, and relearn. I love the way Hall of Fame basketball coach John Wooden states it: "It's what you learn after you know it all that counts."

When I teach and mentor leaders, I remind them that if they stop learning, they stop leading. But if they remain teachable and keep learning, they will be able to keep making an impact as leaders. Whatever your talent happens to be— whether it's leadership, craftsmanship, entrepreneurship, or something else—you will expand it if you keep expecting and striving to learn. Talented individuals with teachable attitudes can become successful people.

TEACHABILITY TRUTHS

The good news is that we don't have to have the talent of a Leonardo da Vinci to be teachable. We just need to have the right attitude about learning. To do that, consider the following truths about teaching:

1. NOTHING IS INTERESTING IF YOU ARE NOT INTERESTED

Management guru Philip B. Crosby wrote in his book *Quality Is Free*:

> There is a theory of human behavior that says people subconsciously retard their own intellectual growth. They come to rely on clichés and habits. Once they reach the age of their own personal comfort with the world, they stop learning and their mind runs on idle for the rest of their days. They may progress organizationally, they may be ambitious and eager, and they may even work night and day. But they learn no more.[1]

It's a shame when people allow themselves to get in a rut and never climb out. They often miss the best that life has to offer. In contrast, teachable people are fully engaged in life. They get excited about things. They are interested in discovery, discussion, application, and growth. There is a definite relationship between passion and potential.

German philosopher Goethe advised, "Never let a day pass without looking at some perfect work of art, hearing some great piece of music and reading, in part, some great book." The more engaged you are, the more interesting life will be. The more interested you are in exploring and learning, the greater your potential for growth.

2. Successful People View Learning Differently from Those Who Are Unsuccessful

Teachable people are always open to new ideas and are willing to learn from anyone who has something to offer. This is one of the things that makes them successful. American journalist Sydney J. Harris wrote, "A winner knows how much he still has to learn, even when he is considered an expert by others. A loser wants to be considered an expert by others, before he has learned enough to know how little he knows." It's all a matter of attitude.

It's truly remarkable how much a person has to learn before he realizes how little he knows. The world is vast, and we are so limited. There is much for us to learn, and we can learn much—as long as we remain teachable.

3. Learning Is Meant to Be a Lifelong Pursuit

It's said that the Roman scholar Cato started to study Greek when he was more than eighty years old. When asked why he was tackling such a difficult task at his age, he replied, "It is the earliest age I have left." Unlike Cato, too many people regard learning as an event instead of a process. Someone told me that only one-third of all adults read an entire book after their last graduation. Why would that be? Because they view education as a period of life, not a way of life!

Learning is an activity that is not restricted by age. It doesn't matter if you're past eighty, like Cato, or haven't yet entered your teens. Every stage of life presents lessons to be learned. We can choose to be teachable and continue to learn them, or we can be closed-minded and stop growing. The decision is ours.

4. Talented People Can Be the Toughest to Teach

The other day I was having lunch with my friend Sam Chand, and we were talking about talent and teachability. Sam mentioned that he had a lot of musical talent. "I can play any type of keyboard, accordion, drums, guitar, saxophone, fiddle," he said. "I can basically play anything. If I hear a tune once, I can play it."

That sounds like a wonderful gift. But Sam said that when he decided to raise his saxophone playing to a new level by taking jazz lessons, he quickly became frustrated. Because he had played by ear and music had always come so easily to him, he didn't possess the patience and perseverance he needed to succeed. Eventually he gave up.

One of the paradoxes of life is that the things that initially *make* you successful are rarely the things that *keep* you successful. You have to remain open to new ideas and be willing to learn new skills. Konrad Höle advises,

> If you cannot be teachable, having talent won't
>   help you.
> If you cannot be flexible, having a goal won't help you.
> If you cannot be grateful, having abundance won't
>   help you.
> If you cannot be mentorable, having a future won't
>   help you.
> If you cannot be durable, having a plan won't help you.
> If you cannot be reachable, having success won't help you.[2]

This may sound strange, but don't let your talent get in the way of your success. Remain teachable.

5. Pride Is the Number One Hindrance to Teachability

Author, trainer, and speaker Dave Anderson believes that the number one cause of management failure is pride. He wrote,

> There are many reasons managers fail. For some, the organization outgrows them. Others don't change with the times . . . A few make poor character choices. They look good for a while but eventually discover they can't get out of their own way. Increasingly more keep the wrong people too long because they don't want to admit they made a mistake or have high turnover become a negative reflection on them. Some failures had brilliant past track records but start using their success as a license to build a fence around what they had rather than continue to risk and stretch to build it to even higher levels. But all these causes for management failure have their root in one common cause: pride. In simplest terms, pride is devastating . . . the pride that inflates your sense of self-worth and distorts your perspective of reality.[3]

While envy is the deadly sin that comes from feelings of *inferiority*, the deadly sin of pride comes from feelings of *superiority*. It creates an arrogance of success, an inflated sense of self-worth accompanied by a distorted perspective of reality. Such an attitude leads to a loss of desire to learn and an unwillingness to change. It makes a person unteachable.

THE PROBLEMS WITH PRIDE

Pride is such a huge barrier to success and the development of talent that we need to examine it in greater detail. Here are just a few of the negative effects of pride as they relate to teachability:

PRIDE CLOSES OUR MINDS TO NEW IDEAS

I've yet to meet a conceited, arrogant, or prideful person who possessed a teachable spirit. How about you? The writer of Proverbs observed, "Do you see a man who is wise in his own eyes? There is more hope for a fool than for him."[4] Teachability in its most fundamental form is a willingness to open our minds to new ideas. Pride prevents that.

PRIDE CLOSES OUR MINDS TO FEEDBACK

Stephen Covey comments, "It takes humility to seek feedback. It takes wisdom to understand it, analyze it, and appropriately act on it." I've already confessed to you that I have not always been a good listener. But I've learned over the years that I cannot do anything of real value alone. Achievement requires teamwork, and none of us is as smart as all of us. Having learned that lesson, I am continually asking members of my team to give me input on my ideas. I find this most valuable before team members or I take action, but I also solicit feedback throughout the process.

PRIDE PREVENTS US FROM ADMITTING MISTAKES

The commanding admiral ordered a group of navy pilots on maneuvers to maintain radio silence. But one young pilot mistakenly turned on his radio and was heard to mutter, "Man, am I fouled up!"

When the admiral heard it, he grabbed the microphone from the radio operator and barked into it, "Will the pilot who broke radio silence identify himself immediately!"

After a long pause, a voice on the radio was heard to say, "I may be fouled up, but I'm not *that* fouled up!"

Fear may keep some people from admitting mistakes, but pride is just as often the cause. The problem is that one of the best ways we grow is by admitting mistakes and learning from them. Writer William Bolitho observed, "The most important thing in life is not to capitalize on our gains. Any fool can do that. The really important thing is to profit from our losses. That requires intelligence; and makes the difference between a man of sense and a fool."

Pride Keeps Us from Making Needed Changes

Anytime we do a job and think we did it well, we become reluctant to make changes to our work. We become dedicated to the status quo instead of progress. Why? Because we have an emotional investment in it. For example, anytime in the past when I've taken a leadership position in which I inherited a staff, I had little reluctance to make changes for the good of the organization. If someone wasn't doing the job and would not or could not grow and improve, I would replace him or her. However, if someone I selected was falling short, I was much slower to make the needed change. Pride caused me to defend what sometimes should not have been defended. When it comes to changing others, we want to do it immediately. But changing ourselves? Not so fast! That's a problem.

HOW TO OVERCOME A PRIDE PROBLEM

If pride is an obstacle to your growth, then you need to take some deliberate and strategic steps to overcome it. That may not be easy. Founding Father Benjamin Franklin observed, "There is perhaps not one of our natural passions so hard to subdue as pride. Beat it down, stifle it, mortify it as much as one pleases, it is still alive. Even if I could conceive that I had completely overcome it, I should probably be proud of my humility." To start the process, here is what I suggest:

1. RECOGNIZE AND ADMIT YOUR PRIDE

The first and most difficult step in overcoming pride is recognizing that it's a problem since those who are bound by it are often unaware of it. To defeat pride, we need to embrace humility, and few desire that. Writer and apologist C. S. Lewis remarked, "If anyone would like to acquire humility, I can, I think, tell him the first step. The first step is to realize that one is proud. And a biggish step, too. At least, nothing whatever can be done before it. If you think you are not conceited, it means you are very conceited indeed."[5]

People have a natural tendency to believe—or to hope—that they are indispensable, that the world will stop and take notice if anything happens to them. But I have to tell you, as someone who has presided over many funerals, life goes on. When someone dies, the family and friends closest to the person grieve. But the rest of the people who attend the reception after the funeral are more worried about the potato salad than the dearly departed. So Kessinger's advice is really good: do your best, but remember that no one is indispensable.

2. EXPRESS GRATITUDE OFTEN

Once when I was chatting with Zig Ziglar, he told me that he thought the least expressed of all virtues is gratitude. I think that is true. I also think it is the most appreciated expression by recipients. I think Oprah Winfrey's suggestion for cultivating gratitude is excellent. She says,

> Keep a grateful journal. Every night, list five things that happened this day that you are grateful for. What it will begin to do is change your perspective of your day and your life. If you can learn to focus on what you have, you will always see that the universe is abundant; you will have more. If you concentrate on what you don't have, you will never have enough.[6]

Therein lies the problem of people filled with selfish pride. They are not grateful because they never think they get as much as they deserve. Expressing gratitude continually helps to break this kind of pride.

3. Laugh at Yourself

I love the Chinese proverb that says, "Blessed are they that laugh at themselves, for they shall never cease to be entertained." People who have the problem of pride rarely laugh at themselves. But engaging in humor at your own expense shows that pride isn't a problem, and it is a way of breaking a pride problem.

There's a story about a judge named Robert S. Gawthorp who had a distinguished career on the bench beginning in 1977 at age forty-four. But he refused to take himself too seriously and maintained his sense of humor. Gawthorp commented, "Just because people stand up when you walk into court and you wear a black dress to work and sit on an elevated chair . . . you have to remind yourself you're just another person who happens to be a lawyer elected to serve as a judge." To remind himself of this, he used to keep a small framed statement near his private courtroom door—a gift from relatives—that said, "To us, you'll always be just the same old jackass."[7]

TAP INTO TEACHABILITY

If you want to expand your talent, you must become teachable. That is the pathway to growth. Futurist and author John Naisbitt believes that "the most important skill to acquire is learning how to learn." Here is what I suggest as you pursue teachability:

1. LEARN TO LISTEN

The first step in teachability is learning to listen. American writer and philosopher Henry David Thoreau wrote, "It takes two to speak the truth—one to speak and one to hear." Being a good listener helps us to know people better, to learn what they have learned, and to show them that we value them as individuals.

Abraham Lincoln was one of the most teachable presidents. When he began his career, he was not a great leader. But he grew into his presidency. He was always an avid listener, and as president, he opened the doors of the White House to anyone who wanted to express an opinion to him. He called these frequent sessions his "public opinion baths." He also asked nearly everyone he met to send him ideas and opinions. As a result, he received hundreds of letters every month—many more than other presidents had received in the past. From this practice, he learned much. And even if he didn't embrace the arguments, he learned more about how the letter writers thought, and he used that knowledge to help him craft his policies and persuade others to adopt them.

As you go through each day, remember that you can't learn if you're always talking. As the old saying goes, "There's a reason you have one mouth but two ears." Listen to others, remain humble, and you will begin to learn things every day that can help you expand your talent.

2. Understand the Learning Process

Sometimes things are painfully obvious and need little explanation. For example, read the following humorous warnings and pieces of advice collected from the military:

- "Aim towards enemy."—Instruction printed on U.S. rocket launcher
- "When the pin is pulled, Mr. Grenade is not our friend."—U.S. Army
- "If the enemy is in range, so are you."—*Infantry Journal*
- "It is generally inadvisable to eject directly over the area you just bombed."—U.S. Air Force Manual
- "If your attack is going too well, you're probably walking into an ambush."—*Infantry Journal*
- "Never tell the platoon sergeant you have nothing to do."—Unknown army recruit
- "Don't draw fire; it irritates the people around you."—Your buddies
- "If you see a bomb technician running, try to keep up with him."—U.S. ammo troop

When things aren't so obvious, it is helpful to understand the learning process in order to learn and grow. Here is how it typically works:

Step 1: Act.
Step 2: Look for your mistakes and evaluate.
Step 3: Search for a way to do it better.
Step 4: Go back to step 1:

Remember, the greatest enemy of learning is knowing, and the goal of all learning is action, not knowledge. If what you are doing does not in some way contribute to what you or others are doing in life, then question its value and be prepared to make changes.

3. Look for and Plan Teachable Moments

If you look for opportunities to learn in every situation, you will be more successful and expand your talent to its potential. But you can also take another step beyond that and actively seek out and plan teachable moments. You can do that by reading books, visiting places that will inspire you, attending events that will prompt you to pursue change, listening to lessons, and spending time with people who will stretch you and expose you to new experiences.

I've had the privilege to spend time with many remarkable people, and the natural reward has been the opportunity to learn. In my personal relationships, I've also gravitated toward people from whom I can learn. My closest friends are people who challenge my thinking—and often change it. They lift me up in many ways. And I've found that I often live out something stated by Spanish philosopher and writer Baltasar Gracian: "Make your friends your teachers and mingle the pleasures of conversation with the advantages of instruction." You can do the same. Cultivate friendships with people who challenge and add value to you, and try to do the same for them. It will change your life.

4. Make Your Teachable Moments Count

Years ago I saw a *Peanuts* cartoon by Charles Schulz that showed Charlie Brown at the beach building a magnificent sand castle. With it completed, he stood back to admire his work, at which point he and his work were engulfed by a downpour that leveled his beautiful castle. In the last frame, he says, "There must be a lesson here, but I don't know what it is."

Unfortunately, that's the way many people feel after a potentially valuable experience. Even people who are strategic about seeking teachable moments can miss the whole point of the experience. I say this because for thirty years I've been a speaker at conferences and workshops—events that are designed to help people learn. But I've found that many people walk away from an event and do very little with what they heard after closing their notebooks. It would be like a jewelry designer going to a gem merchant to buy fine gems, placing them carefully into a case, and then putting that case on the shelf to collect dust. What's the value of acquiring the gems if they're never going to be used?

We tend to focus on learning events instead of the learning process. Because of this, I try to help people take action steps that will help them implement what they learn. I suggest that in their notes, they use a code to mark things that jump out at them:

T indicates you need to spend some time thinking on
    that point.
C indicates something you need to change.
☺ A smiley face means you are doing that thing
    particularly well.
A indicates something you need to apply.

S means you need to share that information with
   someone else.

After the conference I recommend that they create to-do
lists based on what they marked, then schedule time to follow
through.

5. ASK YOURSELF, AM I REALLY TEACHABLE?

I've said it before, but it bears repeating: all the good advice
in the world won't help if you don't have a teachable spirit. To
know whether you are *really* open to new ideas and new ways
of doing things, answer the following questions:

1. Am I open to other people's ideas?
2. Do I listen more than I talk?
3. Am I open to changing my opinion based on new
   information?
4. Do I readily admit when I am wrong?
5. Do I observe before acting on a situation?
6. Do I ask questions?
7. Am I willing to ask a question that will expose my
   ignorance?
8. Am I open to doing things in a way I haven't done
   before?
9. Am I willing to ask for directions?
10. Do I act defensive when criticized, or do I listen
    openly for the truth?

If you answered no to one or more of these questions, then
you have room to grow in the area of teachability. You need
to soften your attitude and learn humility, and remember the

words of John Wooden: "Everything we know we learned from someone else!"

Thomas Edison was the guest of the governor of North Carolina when the politician complimented him on his creative genius.

"I am not a great inventor," countered Edison.

"But you have over a thousand patents to your credit," the governor stated.

"Yes, but about the only invention I can really claim as absolutely original is the phonograph," Edison replied.

"I'm afraid I don't understand what you mean," the governor remarked.

"Well," explained Edison, "I guess I'm an awfully good sponge. I absorb ideas from every course I can, and put them to practical use. Then I improve them until they become of some value. The ideas which I use are mostly the ideas of other people who don't develop them themselves."

What a remarkable description of someone who used teachability to expand his talent! That is what successful people do. That is what all of us should strive to do. Choose to be more teachable.

CHAPTER 11

DEVELOP STRONG CHARACTER

Many people with talent make it into the limelight, but the ones who have neglected to develop strong character rarely stay there long. Absence of strong character eventually topples talent. Why? Because people cannot climb beyond the limitations of their character. Talented people are sometimes tempted to take shortcuts. Character prevents that. Talented people may feel superior and expect special privileges. Character helps them know better. Talented people are praised for what others see them build. Character builds what's inside them. Talented people have the potential to be difference makers. Character makes a difference in them. Talented people are often a gift to the world. Character protects that gift.

THE COMPONENTS OF CHARACTER

People are like icebergs. There's much more to them than meets the eye. When you look at an iceberg, only about fifteen percent is visible—that's talent. The rest—their character—is below the surface, hidden. It's what they think and never share with others. It's what they do when no one is watching them. It's how they react to terrible traffic and other everyday aggravations. It's how they handle failure—and success. The greater their talent is, the greater their need is for strong character "below the surface" to sustain them. If they are too "top heavy" with talent, then they are likely to get into trouble.

No one can expect to succeed without strong character below the surface to protect his talent and sustain him during difficult times. Character holds us steady, no matter how rough the storm becomes. Or to put it another way, as David McLendon did when we spent time together recently, "Character is the pedestal that determines how much weight a person can sustain. If your character is the size of a toothpick, you can only sustain a postage stamp. If your character is as thick as a column, you can sustain a roof."

So what exactly comprises character? Ask a dozen people and you'll get a dozen answers. I believe it boils down to four elements: (1) self-discipline, (2) core values, (3) a sense of identity, and (4) integrity. Let's consider each of them:

1. SELF-DISCIPLINE

At the most basic level, self-discipline is the ability to do what is right even when you don't feel like doing it. Outstanding leaders and achievers throughout history understood this. Greek philosopher Plato asserted, "The first and best victory is to conquer self."

The greatest victories are internal ones. Oswald Sanders, the author of the book on leadership that launched my personal journey as a leader, *Spiritual Leadership*, wrote that the future is with the disciplined. He said that without self-discipline, a leader's other gifts—however great—will never realize their maximum potential. That's true not only of leaders but also of anyone who wants to reach his or her potential. A person must choose to demonstrate character to be successful. The battle for self-discipline is won within. The notable mountain climber Sir Edmund Hillary observed, "It's not the mountains we conquer, but ourselves."

One of the joys of my life is playing golf. I only wish my talent matched my passion! I have had the privilege of playing the East Lake course in Atlanta, home course of golf legend Bobby Jones, considered by some to be the greatest golfer who ever played the game. The club house is filled with pictures of him playing and with many of his championship trophies. Yet many people don't know that Jones's most significant victory was over himself.

Jones began playing golf at age five and won his first tournament at age six. By age twelve he was winning tournaments against adults. But Jones had a temper. His nickname was "Club Thrower." An older gentleman called Grandpa Bart, who had retired from golf but worked in the pro shop, recognized Jones's talent *and* his character issues. After Jones made it to the third round of the U.S. Amateur Championship, the older man advised, "Bobby, you are good enough to win that tournament, but you'll never win until you can control that temper of yours. You miss a shot—you get upset—and then you lose." Jones did master his temper and won his first U.S. Open when he was twenty-one. Grandpa Bart used to say, "Bobby was fourteen when he mastered the game of golf, but he was twenty-one when he mastered himself."

English theologian and orator Henry Parry Liddon observed, "What we do on some great occasion will probably depend on what we already are; and what we are will be the result of previous years of self-discipline." The first step to strong character is conquering self.

2. Core Values

Our core values are the principles we live by every day. They define what we believe and how we live. Ideally, we should write out our core values so that they become a clear beacon we can always use to guide us.

One person I most admire is John Wooden, the Hall of Fame former coach of UCLA's basketball team. When he graduated from grade school at twelve years old, his father gave him a seven-point creed. From that time, Wooden has carried a written copy of that creed with him every day. Here is what it says:

1. Be true to yourself.
2. Help others.
3. Make each day your masterpiece.
4. Drink deeply from good books, especially the Bible.
5. Make friendship a fine art.
6. Build a shelter against a rainy day.
7. Pray for guidance and give thanks for your blessings every day.[1]

I had read about the creed, and when I got to meet Coach Wooden, I asked him about it. Sitting in a restaurant at breakfast, he pulled a copy out of his pocket and showed it to me. Of course, since he has it memorized, he doesn't need to carry a copy with him, but it has been his lifelong practice. Most important, he has always carried it in his heart and sought to live it out every day.

Swiss philosopher Henri Frederic Amiel stated, "The man who has no inner life is the slave of his surroundings." Core values give order and structure to an individual's inner life, and when that inner life is in order, a person can navigate almost anything the world throws at him.

3. A SENSE OF IDENTITY

When it comes to character, each of us must answer the critical question, "Who am I?" That answer often provides the motivation to practice self-discipline. It is fundamental for the identification of core values. And it helps to establish emotional security. Our sense of security—or lack of it—often drives what we do.

American novelist Nathaniel Hawthorne recognized this truth: "No man can for any considerable time wear one face to himself and another to the multitude without finally getting bewildered as to which is the true one." How do you identify yourself? Where does your personal value come from? What is your motivation as it relates to money and power?

If you live with a chip on your shoulder, believe deep down you have no intrinsic value, or see yourself as a victim, you will have a distorted view of yourself and your surroundings. That, in turn, will impact your character. No matter how hard you try, you cannot consistently behave in a way that is inconsistent with how you see yourself. Thus, a strong and accurate sense of identity is essential. To paraphrase author Ruth Barton, people are set up to fail if they envision what they want to do before they figure out what kind of person they should be.

4. INTEGRITY

The final component in strong character is integrity, which is an alignment of values, thoughts, feelings, and actions. People who possess the consistency that comes with strong integrity can be very compelling. In his book *American Scandal*, Pat Williams tells the story of Mahatma Gandhi's trip to England to speak before Parliament. The British government had opposed Indian independence, and Gandhi, one of its most vocal proponents, had often been threatened, arrested, and jailed as a result. Gandhi spoke eloquently and passionately for nearly two hours, after which the packed hall gave him a standing ovation.

Afterward, a reporter asked Gandhi's assistant, Mahadev Desai, how the Indian statesman had been able to deliver such a speech without any notes.

"You don't understand Gandhi," Desai responded. "You see, what he thinks is what he feels. What he feels is what he says. What he says is what he does. What Gandhi feels, what he thinks, what he says, and what he does are all the same. He does not need notes."[2]

When values, thoughts, feelings, and actions are in alignment, a person becomes focused and his character is strengthened. However, when these components aren't aligned, it creates confusion and internal conflict.

Developing talent without developing character is a dead end. It won't take people where they want to go. The lives of people who are long on talent but short on character always get out of balance.

CHARACTER COMMUNICATES

The choice to develop strong character may not be the most important one to make the *most* of your talent. But it is certainly the most important to make sure you don't make the *least* of your talent. You can't really underestimate its impact. Entrepreneur Roger Babson, who founded Babson College and Webber International University, asserted, "A character standard is far more important than even a gold standard. The success of all economic systems is still dependent upon both righteous leaders and righteous people. In the last analysis, our national future depends upon our national character—that is, whether it is spiritually or materially minded."[3]

As I hope I've already made clear, character creates a foundation upon which the structure of your talent and your life can build. If there are cracks in that foundation, you cannot build much. That's why you must first develop within before you can achieve much without. But once you build strong character, it does more than provide a platform for your personal success and the maximization of your talent. It also impacts others and allows you to build with them. It does that through what it communicates to people:

1. CHARACTER COMMUNICATES CONSISTENCY

Cultural anthropologist Margaret Mead stated, "What people say, what people do, and what people say they do are entirely different things." That is true of people who live without character, without integrity. Such people communicate confusion to others. They can say anything they like, but their actions determine the message we receive. It was philosopher-poet Ralph Waldo Emerson who said, "What you do thunders so loudly in my ears I cannot hear what you say."

Amazingly there are people who actually promote this inconsistency. Designer Ralph Lauren was quoted as saying, "The crux of a person's identity . . . resides in the trappings, not in the person himself . . . One needn't be well read, so long as one surrounds himself with books. One needn't play the piano, so long as one has a piano. In short, one can be whoever one wants to be. Or—more accurately—one can seem to be whoever one wants to be."⁴ While one may be able to make an *impression* with "trappings," the real person always comes through in the end. Impressions are like shadows—they disappear when a strong enough light is shone on them. Character is the genuine article—and the more you shine light on it, the more of its details you can see. Character shows that who you are and who you appear to be are one and the same, and that, according to Greek philosopher Socrates, is the first key to greatness.

2. Character Communicates Choices

Earlier in this chapter I mentioned that Bobby Jones needed to overcome a terrible temper to succeed at golf. Not only did Jones do that, but he actually became a model of sportsmanship and character. Both could be seen in his play. During the final playoff of a U.S. Open tournament, Jones's ball ended up in the rough just off the fairway. As he set up to play his shot, he accidentally caused his ball to move. He immediately turned to the marshals and announced the foul. The marshals discussed the situation among themselves. They hadn't seen the ball move. Neither did anyone in the gallery. They left it up to Jones whether to take the penalty stroke, which he did.

Later, when a marshal commended Jones on his high level of integrity, Jones replied, "Do you commend a bank robber for not robbing a bank? No, you don't. This is how the game of golf should be played at all times." Jones lost the match that day—by one stroke. But he didn't lose his integrity. His character was so well-known that the United States Golf Association's sportsmanship award came to be named the Bob Jones Award.[5]

It's an interesting paradox. Our character creates our choices, yet our choices create our character. Author and speaker Margaret Jensen observed, "Character is the sum total of all our everyday choices. Our character today is a result of our choices yesterday. Our character tomorrow will be a result of our choices today. To change your character, change your choices. Day by day, what you think, what you choose, and what you do is who you become." Once you get a handle on the character of a person, you can understand his choices and even predict what they will be.

3. Character Communicates Influence

Today, many people try to demand respect. They believe that influence should be granted to them simply because they have position, wealth, or recognition. However, respect and influence must be earned over time, and they are built and sustained by character. First and foremost, influence is based on character. U.S. Army general J. Lawton Collins asserted, "No matter how brilliant a man may be, he will never engender confidence in his subordinates and associates if he lacks simple honesty and moral courage."

I've taught leadership for more than three decades, and I've written many books on it. During that time I've tried to help people develop skills that will benefit them as leaders. However, all the skills in the world won't assist someone whose character is hopelessly flawed. Experienced leaders understand this. Author Stephen Covey wrote,

> If I try to use human influence strategies and tactics of how to get other people to do what I want, to work better, to be more motivated to like me and each other while my character is fundamentally flawed, marked by duplicity or insincerity then, in the long run, I cannot be successful. My duplicity will breed distrust, and everything I do—even using so-called good human relations techniques will be perceived as manipulative.[6]

It simply makes no difference how good the rhetoric is or even how good the intentions are; if there is little or no trust, there is no foundation for permanent success.

Character cannot be inherited. It cannot be bought. It is impossible to weigh, and it cannot be physically touched. It can be built, but only slowly. And without it, one cannot lead others.

4. CHARACTER COMMUNICATES LONGEVITY

If you want to know how long it will take to get to the top, consult a calendar. If you want to know how long it can take to fall to the bottom, try a stopwatch. Character determines which will happen. Dreams become shattered, possibilities are lost, organizations crumble, and people are hurt when a person doesn't have character protecting his talent. Character provides the opportunity for longevity in any career, any relationship, and any worthwhile goal.

Author and pastor J. R. Miller wrote, "The only thing that walks back from the tomb with the mourners and refuses to be buried is the character of a man. This is true. What a man is, survives him. It can never be buried." If you want your talent to last, and you want to sleep well at night, depend upon good character. Asked about the secret of a long and happy life, Coach John Wooden remarked on his ninetieth birthday, "There is no pillow as soft as a clear conscience." Character protects your talent, and it also guards you from regret.

CHARACTER BUILDING

Never forget that talent is a gift—either you have it or you don't—but character is a choice. If you want it, you must develop it. Here's how:

1. Don't Give Up or Give In to Adversity

It takes character to weather life's storms. At the same time, adversity develops character. Author and activist Helen Keller, who could not hear or see, remarked, "Character cannot be developed in ease and quiet. Only through experience of trial and suffering can the soul be strengthened, vision cleared, ambition inspired, and success achieved."

Anyone who does what he must only when he is in the mood or when it is convenient isn't going to develop his talent or become successful. The core foundation of character is doing what you don't want to do to get what you want. It is paying a higher price than you wanted to for something worthwhile. It is standing up for your principles when you know someone is going to try to knock you down. Every time you face adversity and come through it with your core values affirmed and your integrity intact, your character becomes stronger.

German philosopher-poet Johann Wolfgang von Goethe observed, "Talent can be cultivated in tranquility; character only in the rushing stream of life." The irony is that if you have never experienced the resistance of the rushing stream, then whatever talent you have cultivated in tranquility may not survive. If you want your talent to take you far, then don't quit under duress. Don't give up in the midst of a storm. Don't bail out in the middle of conflict. Wait until the trouble is behind you before assessing whether it's time to change course or stop. Do that, and you may have additional opportunities to develop your talent.

2. Do the Right Thing

Doing the right thing doesn't come naturally to any of us. As America's first president, George Washington, said, "Few men have virtue enough to withstand the highest bidder." Yet that is what we must do to develop the kind of character that will sustain us.

It's not easy to do the right thing when the wrong thing is expedient. Molière commented, "Men are alike in their promises. It is only in their deeds that they differ. The difference in their deeds is simple: People of character do what is right regardless of the situation." It's not easy to do the right thing when it will cost you. It's not easy to do the right thing when no one but you will know. But it's in those moments that a person's character becomes strong. Civil rights leader Martin Luther King Jr. asserted this:

On some positions cowardice asks the question, is it safe? Expediency asks the question, is it politic? Vanity asks the question, is it popular? But conscience asks the question, is it right? And there comes a time when one must take a position that is neither safe, nor politic, nor popular but he must take it because conscience tells him it is right.[7]

That is the bottom line. Are you going to do what's right?

One way I've tried to control my natural bent to do wrong is to ask myself some questions:

1. Am I hiding something?
2. Am I hurting anyone?
3. How does it look from the other person's point of view?
4. Have I discussed this face-to-face?
5. What would I tell my child to do?

If you do the right thing—and keep doing it—even if it doesn't help you move ahead with your talent in the short term, it will protect you and serve you well in the long term. Character builds—and it builds you. Or as Dr. Dale Bronner, a board member of my nonprofit organization EQUIP, puts it, "Honesty is not something you do; honesty is who you are."

3. Take Control of Your Life

I have observed that the people with the weakest character tend to place the blame on their circumstances. They often claim that poor upbringing, financial difficulties, the unkindness of others, or other circumstances have made them victims. It's true that in life we must face many things outside our control. But know this: while your circumstances *are* beyond your control, your character *is not*. Your character is always your choice.

People can no sooner blame their character on their circumstances than they can blame their looks on a mirror. Developing character is your personal responsibility. It cannot be given to you; you must earn it. Commit yourself to its development because it will protect your talent. Every time you make a character-based decision, you take another step toward success. The process begins with deciding to make good character your goal and to stop making excuses. French writer François La Rochefoucauld asserted, "Almost all our faults are more pardonable than the methods we think up to hide them." The process continues with the determination to manage that decision every day.

You have God-given talent; develop it. You have opportunity before you; pursue it. You have a future that is bright; look forward to it. But above all else, you have the potential to become a person of character; follow through with it. Character, more than anything else, will protect everything in your life that you hold dear.

CHAPTER 12

CULTIVATE GOOD RELATIONSHIPS

In his book *My Personal Best*, John Wooden wrote, "There is a choice you have to make in everything you do, so keep in mind that in the end, the choice you make makes you."[1] Nowhere is this more evident than in your relationships. Nothing will influence your talent as much as the important relationships in your life. Surround yourself with people who add value to you and encourage you, and your talent will go in a positive direction. Spend time with people who constantly drain you, pull you in the wrong direction, or try to knock you down, and it will be almost impossible for your talent to take flight. People can trace the successes and failures in their lives to their most significant relationships.

THE IMPACT OF RELATIONSHIPS

I think many people mistakenly minimize the impact other people can have on their lives. My parents understood the influence of relationships. Today as I look back on my formative years, I see how intentional they were about who we spent time with and who we selected as our friends. My parents made our house the place to be in the neighborhood. We had a pool table, a Ping-Pong table, and a chemistry set in our basement. We had a shuffleboard court, a basketball court, and a Wiffle ball diamond in our yard. Everybody wanted to come to our house. And that was the strategy. My parents wanted to be able to know the kids we played with. Typical of the times (it was the 1950s and 1960s), my mom didn't work outside the home, so she was always there to keep an eye on us.

Mom was always on the periphery of our play, fixing us lunch or a cold drink, putting bandages on cuts, and observing the interaction and behavior of each person. Every now and then she would ask my brother, Larry, my sister, Trish, or me about a particular friend. As children, we had no idea of the importance of associating with good kids rather than bad ones, but our parents did. They made sure the influences on our lives were positive.

Years later when I was an adult and I spent several hours a week counseling people, I learned through daily observation what my parents knew. Almost all our sorrows can be traced to relationships with the wrong people and our joys to relationships with the right people.

THE IMPACT OF SOME RELATIONSHIPS

The relationships in our lives really do make or break us. They either lift us up or take us down. They add, or they subtract.

They help to give us energy, or they take it away. Here's what I mean:

SOME RELATIONSHIPS TAKE FROM US

There are a couple of good ways to tell whether a relationship is positive or negative. The first is to note whether a person makes you feel better or worse about yourself. The second relates to how much energy the relationship requires. Let's face it, some relationships feel as if they could suck the life out of you. In his book *High-Maintenance Relationships*, Les Parrott offers a straightforward quiz that can help you tell whether someone in your life is a negative person who takes energy from you. Answer yes or no to each of the following questions:

_____ Do you feel especially anxious when a particular person has called and left a message for you to return the call?

_____ Have you recently been dealing with a relationship that drains you of enthusiasm and energy?

_____ Do you sometimes dread having to see or talk to a particular person at work or in a social situation?

_____ Do you have a relationship in which you give more than you get in return?

_____ Do you find yourself second-guessing your own performance as a result of an interaction with this person?

_____ Do you become more self-critical in the presence of this person?

_____ Is your creativity blocked, or is your clarity of mind hampered somewhat, by the lingering discomfort of having to deal with a difficult person?

_____ Do you try to calm yourself after being with this person by

_____ eating more, biting your nails, or engaging in some other unhealthy habit?

_____ Do you ever have imaginary conversations with this person or mental arguments in which you defend yourself or try to explain your side of a conflict?

_____ Have you become more susceptible to colds, stomach problems, or muscle tension since having to deal with this difficult person?

_____ Do you feel resentful that this person seems to treat other people better than she or he treats you?

_____ Do you find yourself wondering why this person singles you out for criticism but rarely acknowledges things you do well?

_____ Have you thought about quitting your job as a result of having to interact with this difficult person?

_____ Have you noticed that you are more irritable or impatient with people you care about because of leftover frustrations from your interaction with this difficult person?

_____ Are you feeling discouraged that this person has continued to drain you of energy despite your efforts to improve the relationship?

Les says that if you answered yes to ten or more of the questions, then you are certainly in a high-maintenance relationship.[2]

I don't mean to imply that only negative relationships require you to put energy into them. All relationships require you to give *some* energy. Relationships don't cultivate and sustain themselves. The question is, how much energy do they require? And do they give anything in return? For example, some of the positive relationships that require a tremendous amount of energy in my life include:

- **My family**—every family has ups and down, but that's okay; that's what it means to be in a family.
- **My inner circle of friends**—these people get everything I've got, and they give their all too; that's what friendship is all about.
- **My team**—leadership begins with a serving attitude; I always try to give more than I receive.
- **Those less fortunate than I am**—every year I travel to developing countries to train leaders and add value to people through EQUIP, my nonprofit organization.

If a relationship requires you to expend energy some of the time, that's normal. If a relationship saps your energy all the time, then that relationship has a negative effect on you. You may be able to see its effects in many areas of your life. It dilutes your talent because it robs you of energy that you could be using toward your best gifts and skills. It distracts you from your purpose. And it detracts from your best efforts. In the long run, a negative relationship cannot influence your talent in a positive direction.

Some Relationships Add to Us

Some relationships clearly make us better. They energize, inspire, and validate us. They lift us up and give us joy. We should view the people in these relationships as friends and value them highly. Helen Keller remarked, "My friends have made the story of my life. In a thousand ways they have turned my limitations into beautiful privileges, and enabled me to walk serene and happy in the shadow cast by my deprivation."[3]

Not long ago, I sat down and listed the types of people who add value to my life and give me energy. Here is what I wrote:

1. **My family**—the best moments with my family are *my* best moments.
2. **Creative people**—they unleash creativity within me like no others.
3. **Successful people**—I love to hear their stories.
4. **Encouraging people**—encouragement is like oxygen to my soul.
5. **Fun people**—laughter always lifts my spirit.
6. **Good thinkers**—conversations with them are my favorite things.
7. **My team**—they always add value to me.
8. **Learners**—interested people are interesting people.

Positive relationships take us to a higher level. They encourage us and bring out the best in us. They make us better than we otherwise would be without them. They are some of life's greatest gifts!

Some Relationships Are Pivotal to Our Lives

Throughout a lifetime, people are in contact with thousands of people in varying levels of relationships. Most have a very limited impact on us. But a few relationships have such a tremendous impact that they change the course of our lives. They are pivotal to who we are and what we do. I don't think anyone can try to create one of these relationships. I call them simply God's gift to me. I don't deserve them—but I do need them. People with whom I have enjoyed this kind of relationship give beyond reason and lift me up to a level I *could not* achieve without them.

Tom Phillippe is one such friend. Tom and I have been friends for more than thirty years. We have traveled the world together, yet we also enjoy just sitting at home talking with no other agenda. Not long ago a group of Tom's friends got together with him to celebrate his seventieth birthday. Each of us had the chance to tell the others how Tom has affected our lives. I wrote what I wanted to say and read it to the group:

> Tom has loved me unconditionally. Victor Hugo said, "The supreme happiness of life is being loved in spite of yourself." Tom has also loved me continually. In 1980, he encouraged me to join the Wesleyan denomination. In 1981, he began assisting me in starting leadership conferences. He gave me an opportunity to enter the business world. He managed my personal development organization when time would not allow me to do it. He financially kept my nonprofit organization alive in its beginning days. Today it trains millions of leaders internationally. One of God's gifts to me was Tom's friendship.

I then closed with a poem called "Your Name Is Written . . . at the Top of My List." Tom has changed my life forever. He has been a lifter in so many areas of my life. If you ever encounter someone who has that impact on you, fight to preserve that relationship, show your gratitude often, and give whatever you can in return.

FIVE SIGNS OF A GOOD RELATIONSHIP

Relationships at the secure level validate us and help us to become more comfortable with who we are and to discover our gifts and talents. Good relationships add value to us so that our talent is actually enhanced. Our good friends tell us the truth in a supportive way. They keep us grounded. If we start to get off course, they help keep us on track. They encourage us when we're down and inspire us to go higher. A few good relationships can make all the difference in where a talented person ends up in life.

As you engage in relationships, try to find people with whom you can build relationships that are mutually beneficial. Here are the signs that a relationship is headed toward that level:

1. MUTUAL ENJOYMENT

In good relationships, people spend time together just for the enjoyment of being together. What they do is not of significance. For example, my wife, Margaret, and I often run errands together. What's enjoyable about dropping off the dry cleaning, buying groceries, or picking up items at a neighborhood shop? Nothing—except spending time with her.

I think when many of us were kids, we intuitively understood the value of spending time with someone special. Do you remember how it felt to sit on the lap of your mother or father when you were small? Or how excited you got when a favorite uncle or a grandparent came to visit? Or how it felt when you first started dating? Unfortunately, the busyness and pressures of life often cause us to forget what a joy this can be. I've always valued time with Margaret. Now that she and I are grandparents, time with people I love means even more to me. Try not to let the stresses of life make you lose track of that.

2. RESPECT

When you value someone on the front end of a relationship, you earn respect on the back end. And that's foundational to all good relationships. When do people respect you? When you don't let obstacles or circumstances become more important to you than the relationship. When the pressure is on and you still treat them with patience and respect. When the relationship is struggling and you are willing to work hard to protect and preserve it. That's when you have proven worthy of others' respect. Respect is almost always built on difficult ground.

Proverbs, the book of wisdom in the Bible, teaches about the strength of relationships:

- Friends are scarce (18:24).
- Friends will not jump ship when the going gets rough (17:17).
- Friends will be available for counsel (27:9).
- Friends will speak the truth to you (27:6).
- Friends will sharpen you (27:17).
- Friends will be sensitive to your feelings (26:18–19).
- Friends will stick with you (16:28; 18:24).

People who respect each other and build a good relationship enjoy all of these benefits of friendship.

3. SHARED EXPERIENCES

Going through a significant experience with another person creates a mutual bond. The experience can be positive or negative. Families come together and enjoy reminiscing about vacations they took years before (often the more disastrous, the more fondly remembered!). Colleagues build relationships as they work together on high-pressure projects. Soldiers talk about the bond that occurs as they train together and how it only increases if they go to war together. We all need others to lean on and to celebrate with. Shared experiences give us those opportunities.

I still remember vividly my father taking me out of school when I was ten years old so that I could accompany him on a business trip. At the time, he was a district superintendent in our denomination, which meant that he was a pastor and leader to many pastors of local churches in our region. Dad and I packed for the trip and traveled from town to town by car. As we rode along, we talked. As he met with the various pastors, I watched him encouraging them. It not only created a special bond between us, but it modeled the kind of work with people that I would one day be doing myself. It was an experience I will treasure until the day I die.

4. Trust

Ralph Waldo Emerson wrote, "The glory of friendship is not in the outstretched hand, nor the kindly smile, nor the joy of companionship; it is in the spiritual inspiration that comes to one when he discovers that someone else believes in him and is willing to trust him."[4] Trust is both a joy of relationships and a necessary component. In my book *Winning with People*, I described the Bedrock Principle, which says, "Trust is the foundation of any relationship." Nothing is more important in relationships. If you don't have trust, you don't have much of a relationship.

5. Reciprocity

All relationships experience ebb and flow. Sometimes one person is the primary giver. Sometimes the other person is.

But relationships that continue to be one-sided will not remain solid. When they continue to be out of balance, they become unstable and often unhealthy. If you want the relationship to continue, you will need to make changes. Here's how it works:

- When you are getting the better of the relationship, changes must be made.
- When the other person is getting the better part, changes must be made.
- When you're both getting an equally good deal, continue as before.

Friendships are like bank accounts. You cannot continue to draw on them without making deposits. If either of you becomes overdrawn and it stays that way, then the relationship won't last.

Good relationships must be beneficial to both parties. Each person has to put the other first, and both have to benefit. Hall of Fame football coach Vince Lombardi described this when he was asked what made a winning team. He observed,

> There are a lot of coaches with good ball clubs who know the fundamentals and have plenty of discipline but still don't win the game. Then you come to the third ingredient: if you're going to play together as a team, you've got to care for one another. You've got to *love*[5] each other. Each player has to be thinking about the next guy and saying to himself, "If I don't block that man, Paul is going to get his legs broken. I have to do my job in order that he can do his." The difference between mediocrity and greatness is the feeling these guys have for each other.[5]

Good relationships are always win-win. If both people aren't winning, then the relationship isn't good, and it won't last.

RELATIONSHIP REVIEW

If you desire to become successful in the area of relationships—a person whose relationships influence him or her in a positive direction—then here is what I suggest you do:

1. IDENTIFY THE MOST IMPORTANT PEOPLE IN YOUR LIFE

Who are the significant people in your life, the people you spend the most time with, the people whose opinions mean the most to you? These people are your greatest influencers. You need to identify who they are before you can assess how they are influencing your talent.

2. ASSESS WHETHER THEY ARE INFLUENCING YOU IN THE RIGHT DIRECTION

Once you have identified the people who are influencing you, you would be wise to discern *how* they are influencing you. The easiest way to do that is to ask the following questions about each person:

What does he or she think of me? People tend to become what the most important person in their lives believes they can be. Think about small children. If their parents tell them they are losers, stupid, or worthless, they believe they are. If their parents tell them they are smart, attractive, and valuable, they believe they are. We embrace the opinions of people we respect.

Ralph Waldo Emerson asserted, "Every man is entitled to

be valued by his best moments."[6] If you want to be influenced in a positive direction, you need to spend time with people who think positively about you. They need to believe in you.

What does he or she think of my future? Novelist Mark Twain advised, "Keep away from people who try to belittle your ambitions."[7] Do the most important people in your life envision a positive future for you? Do they see great things ahead of you?

Margaret, my wife, has given me many wonderful gifts during the course of our relationship. One that I cherish is the ministry log book she gave me the year before we were married, knowing that a pastoral career was ahead of me. In it, I could record my activities such as sermon topics, weddings, and funerals. It is a record of my life leading local churches. But I value it most for something she wrote in it in 1968. It said simply,

> John,
>   You're going to accomplish great things.
>   Love,
>   Margaret

Her few words weren't poetic or profound, but they communicated her confidence in me and her belief in my future. And she has demonstrated that belief in me every day of our marriage.

How does he or she behave toward me in difficult times? There's an old saying: "In prosperity our friends know us. In adversity we know our friends." Haven't you found that to be true? When times are tough and you're having difficulties, a friend who is influencing you in the right direction is . . .

SLOW TO	BUT QUICK TO
Suspect	Trust
Condemn	Justify
Offend	Defend
Expose	Shield
Reprimand	Forbear
Belittle	Appreciate
Demand	Give
Provoke	Help
Resent	Forgive

When you get knocked down, good friends don't kick you while you're down or say, "I told you so." They pick you up and help you keep going.

What does he or she bring out of me? British prime minister Benjamin Disraeli observed, "The greatest good you can do for another is not just to share your riches but to reveal to him his own." That is really the essence of positive relationships that influence people to rise up and reach their potential. They see the best in you and encourage you to strive for it.

Author William Arthur Ward remarked, "A true friend knows your weaknesses but shows you your strengths; feels your fears but fortifies your faith; sees your anxieties but frees your spirit; recognizes your disabilities but emphasizes your possibilities."[8] That's what positive relationships should do.

3. If Your Friends Aren't Friends, Then Make New Friends

If the people close to you are dragging you down, then it may be time to make some changes. Speaker Joe Larson remarked, "My friends didn't believe that I could become a successful speaker. So I did something about it. I went out and found me some new friends!"

When you really think about it, the things that matter most in life are the relationships we develop. Remember:

You may build a beautiful house, but eventually it will
    crumble.
You may develop a fine career, but one day it will be over.
You may save a great sum of money, but you can't take it
    with you.
You may be in superb health today, but in time it will
    decline.
You may take pride in your accomplishments, but
    someone will surpass you.
Discouraged? Don't be, for the one thing that really
    matters, lasts forever—your friendships.

Life is too long to spend it with people who pull you in the wrong direction. And it's too short not to invest in others. Your relationships will define you. And they will influence your talent—one way or the other. Choose wisely.

CHAPTER 13

COMMIT TO RESPONSIBILITY

Nothing adds "muscle" to talent like responsibility. It lifts talent to a new level and increases its stamina. However, as I consider the choices that help make someone successful, I realize that responsibility is often the last choice people desire to make. The result is "flabby" talent that fails to perform and never realizes its potential. How sad for the person who fails to take responsibility. How sad for others. Author and editor Michael Korda said, "Success on any major scale requires you to accept responsibility . . . In the final analysis, the one quality that all successful people have . . . is the ability to take on responsibility."[1] If you desire success, make responsibility your choice.

THE STRENGTH OF RESPONSIBILITY

We live in a culture that overvalues talent and undervalues responsibility. If you doubt that, then examine the way we treat our athletes. When athletes are in high school and college, their reckless or irresponsible acts are often overlooked in proportion to the talent they display on the court or playing field. What a disservice to them. Responsibility actually strengthens talent and increases the opportunity for long-term success. Here is how it helps:

1. RESPONSIBILITY PROVIDES THE FOUNDATION OF SUCCESS

Sociology professor Tony Campolo points out the importance of having a strong sense of responsibility, especially in a culture like ours that values freedom. Of the American system, he wrote,

> While I think it lays down the principles that make for the best political system ever devised, the Constitution has one basic flaw. It clearly delineates the Bill of Rights, but it nowhere states a Bill of Responsibilities. . . . Government that ensures people of their rights but fails to clearly spell out their responsibilities, fails to call them to be the kind of people God wants them to be.[2]

I agree wholeheartedly with Campolo's call for responsibility. In fact, for years I've taught leaders that as they move up the ladder and take on greater responsibility, their rights actually *decrease*. Leadership requires sacrifice. And while taking on responsibility is also a sacrifice, it is one that brings tremendous rewards.

I once had the opportunity to spend time on the aircraft carrier USS *Enterprise*. I received a tour of the ship and listened to many officers explain the various tasks and functions of the fifty-five hundred people aboard the ship. What struck me was that the officers' messages had a common theme. They talked about the importance of their area to the overall mission of the

ship and how the responsibility for those functions was shoul-
dered by a bunch of nineteen-year-old sailors. The officers
made these statements with pride.

One officer told me about leading a former gang member under his command. The young man had been given the
choice of jail or the navy. The troubled youth became an effective part of the team and was then the leader of his squad. His
proudest moments in the military, this officer said, came from
helping troubled kids to succeed.

What turned kids into productive citizens and trouble-
makers into leaders? Responsibility! When they entered the
service, they became immersed in a culture of responsibility.
That culture demanded that they act accordingly, that they
become responsible and productive. When people respond to a
call for responsibility by giving their best, good things happen.

The young men and women I met had made the choice to
embrace responsibility, and it was creating success for them in
the military. It will continue to provide a foundation for their
success in the coming years, no matter what they do.

2. Responsibility, Handled Correctly, Leads to More Responsibility

Years ago the editor of the *Bellefontaine* [Ohio] *Examiner*,
Gene Marine, sent a new sports reporter to cover a big game.
The reporter returned to the paper with no report.

"Where's the story?" asked Marine.

"No report," replied the reporter.

"What?" growled Marine. "And why not?"

"No game."

"No game? What happened?" quizzed the editor.

"The stadium collapsed."

"Then where's the report on the collapse of the stadium?" demanded Marine.

"That wasn't my assignment, sir."

People who handle their responsibilities well get the opportunity to handle additional responsibilities. Those who don't, don't.

3. RESPONSIBILITY MAXIMIZES ABILITY AND OPPORTUNITY

During the Major League Baseball players' strike of 1994, many trading card manufacturers found themselves in a tough spot. Pinnacle Brands, however, was determined not to lay off any of its employees. Yet the company had to make some changes to be able to pay everyone until business picked up again. So what did management do? Placed the responsibility on the workers for finding ways to replace the $40 million in lost revenue. CEO Jerry Meyer told his employees, "I'm not going to save your jobs. You're going to save your jobs. You know what you can change and what you can do differently."

The people did not let themselves down. A custodian reported that the company spent $50,000 on sodas for conference rooms, an expense that was cut. A finance department worker found a way to streamline trademark searches that saved the company $100,000. A PR manager signed a deal to distribute pins at the Olympics, generating $20 million. In the end, Pinnacle was the only one of the top trading card manufacturers that didn't lay off workers during the baseball strike.[3]

Responsibility has value, not just in hard times, but at all times. It increases our abilities and gives us opportunities. One reason it does is that it causes us to take action, to make things happen. On the job, we need to take responsibility, not just for what we're assigned, but for the contribution we make.

For example, if you're in business, at the end of every day you should ask yourself, *Did I make a profit for my employer today?* If the answer is no, then you may be in trouble. Take responsibility for being a contributor. Every worker needs to be an asset to the company, not an expense.

Author Richard L. Evans remarked, "It is priceless to find a person who will take responsibility, who will finish and follow through to the final detail—to know when someone has accepted an assignment that it will be effectively, conscientiously completed."[4] When leaders find responsible people, they reward them with opportunities and resources that help them to become more effective.

4. RESPONSIBILITY, OVER TIME, BUILDS A SOLID REPUTATION

Responsible people enjoy an increasingly better reputation. And that is one of the greatest assets of sustained responsibility. Others discover what they can expect from you, and they know they can depend on you. You're solid.

In contrast, the longer you know a person who lacks responsibility, the *less* you trust him. A person may try to compartmentalize his life—taking responsibility in one area and shirking it in another—but in the long run it doesn't work. Irresponsibility, left unchecked, inevitably grows and spreads into other areas of a person's life.

A general from American history whose reputation continued to grow was Dwight D. Eisenhower. In fact, his reputation became so strong that it got him elected president. Though he was only an average president, he was an excellent general. One reason was his willingness to take responsibility for his decisions.

During World War II, Eisenhower was responsible for planning the D-Day invasion of Normandy, France. Giving the okay for the assault was a painful decision, one he knew would lead to the deaths of many servicemen. Yet he also knew that if it was successful, it would be a pivotal point in the war against the Nazis.

Pat Williams, in his book *American Scandal*, wrote that in the hours prior to the assault, Eisenhower handwrote a press release that would be used in the event of the invasion's failure. It read,

> Our landings have failed . . . and I have withdrawn the troops. My decision to attack at this time and this place was based upon the best information available. The troops, the air, and the Navy did all that bravery and devotion to duty could do. If any blame or fault attaches to the attempt, it is mine alone.[5]

Eisenhower had determined that he would take responsibility for whatever happened. That mind-set earned the admiration of his fellow officers, his soldiers, and citizens alike.

If you want others to trust you, to give you greater opportunities and resources to develop and strengthen your talent, and to partner with you, then embrace responsibility and practice it faithfully in every area of your life.

RESPONSIBILITY IN ACTION

There's no way for me to know your personal history in regard to responsibility. Maybe assuming responsibility has been a problem for you. Or you may have a strong sense of responsibility, and you never drop the ball. Either way, please review the following steps to help you become more successful when it comes to responsibility:

1. Start Wherever You Are

Greek philosopher Aristotle observed, "We become what we are as persons by the decisions that we ourselves make." Each time you make a responsible decision, you become a more responsible person. Even if your track record hasn't been good up to now, you can change. Successful people take personal responsibility for their actions and their attitudes. They show response-ability—the ability to choose a correct response, no matter what situation they face. Responsibility is always a choice, and only you can make it.

If being responsible has not been one of your strengths, then start small. You can't start from anyplace other than where you are. I think you'll find that when it comes to responsibility, the best helping hand you will ever find is at the end of your arm.

2. Choose Your Friends Wisely

Since I've devoted an entire chapter to relationships and how they influence talent, I don't need to say very much here. Heed the advice of trainer and consultant Kevin Eikenberry, who says, "Look carefully at the closest associations in your life, for that is the direction you are heading." If you have started your journey on the road to responsibility, just make sure that you have the right traveling companions. You will find it difficult or impossible to be responsible when you spend most of your time with irresponsible people.

3. Stop Blaming Others

The sales manager of a dog food company asked his sales team how they liked the company's new advertising program.

"Great!" they replied. "The best in the business."

"What do you think of the product?" he asked.

"Fantastic," they replied.

"How about the sales force?" he asked.

They were the sales force, so of course they responded positively, saying they were the best.

"Okay then," the manager asked, "so if we have the best brand, the best packaging, the best advertising program, and the best sales force, why are we in seventeenth place in our industry?"

After an awkward silence, one of the salesmen stated, "It's those darned dogs—they just won't eat the stuff!"

If you want to be successful, you need to stop blaming others, take a good look in the mirror, and take responsibility for your own life. Oprah Winfrey says, "My philosophy is that not only are you responsible for your life, but doing the best at this moment puts you in the best place for the next moment."[6]

Ron French of the Gannett News Service wrote that failing to take responsibility has become pervasive in America:

Ducking responsibility has become an American pastime. We all have learned to play the blame game, where the seven deadly sins are acceptable syndromes, and criminals are victims. From lifelong smokers suing tobacco companies, to students rationalizing cheating, we've become a nation of whiners and cry babies. "It's part of the American character nowadays," says Charles Sykes, author of *A Nation of Victims*.

"We've gone from a society of people who were self-reliant to a people who inherently refuse to accept responsibility."[7]

People who think others are responsible for their situation assign the blame to various individuals, institutions, or entities. Some fault society or "the times." Some point at the system or "the man." (Criminals serving time in prison are notorious for blaming others and declaring their innocence.) Others rail against the previous generation as the cause of their problems. But do you know why? Cartoonist Doug Larson observed, "The reason people blame things on previous generations is that there's only one other choice."

Some of the best advice you could follow on this subject came from President Theodore Roosevelt: "Do what you can with what you have, where you are." That's all any of us can do. Don't make excuses. Don't look for others to blame. Just focus on the present and do your best. And if you make a mistake or fail, find whatever fault you can inside yourself and try to do better the next time around.

4. LEARN RESPONSIBILITY'S MAJOR LESSONS

There are four core lessons we need to learn if we want to display the kind of responsibility that makes us successful. The lessons are simple and obvious. They are also very difficult to master:

Recognize that gaining success means practicing self-discipline. The first victory we must win is over ourselves. We must learn to control ourselves. You can use any incentive you want to do this: the desire to follow moral or ethical values, rewards for delayed gratification, even the threat of public exposure. Business executive John Weston commented, "I've always tried to live with the following simple rule: Don't do what you wouldn't feel comfortable reading about in the newspaper the next day." Every time you stop yourself from doing what you shouldn't or start yourself doing what you should, you are strengthening your self-discipline and increasing your capacity for responsibility.

What you start, finish. There are two kinds of people in the world: those who do and those who might. Responsible people follow through. If they make a commitment, they see it through. They finish. And that is how others evaluate them. Are they dependable or not? Can I rely on them? Writer Ben Ames Williams observed, "Life is the acceptance of responsibilities or their evasion; it is a business of meeting obligations or avoiding them. To every man the choice is continually being offered, and by the manner of his choosing you may fairly measure him."

Know when others are depending on you. Talent does not succeed on its own. (I'll discuss that in detail in the next chapter.) If you desire to be successful, you will need others. Sometimes you will have to depend on them. And there will be times they need to depend on you. In my book *The 17 Indisputable Laws of Teamwork*, I wrote about the Law of Countability, which says, "Teammates must be able to count on each other when it counts."

The first step in making yourself the kind of person others can depend on is being dependable. The second is taking the focus off yourself and becoming aware that others are depending on you. Having the *intention* to be responsible isn't enough. Your *actions* need to come through.

Don't expect others to step in for you. The following challenge was issued to the 1992 graduating class of the University of South Carolina by Alexander M. Saunders Jr., chief judge of the South Carolina Court of Appeals:

As responsibility is passed to your hands, it will not do, as you live the rest of your life, to assume that someone else will bear the major burdens, that someone else will demonstrate the key convictions, that someone else will run for office, that someone else will take care of the poor, that someone else will visit the sick, protect civil rights, enforce the law, preserve culture, transmit value, maintain civilization, and defend freedom.

You must never forget that what you do not value will not be valued, that what you do not remember will not be remembered, that what you do not change will not be changed, that what you do not do will not be done. You can, if you will, craft a society whose leaders, business and political, are less obsessed with the need for money. It is not really a question of what to do but simply the will to do it.

Many people sit back and wait for someone else to step up and take responsibility. Sometimes that is because of weak character—laziness, lack of resolve, and so on. But more often it comes from poor judgment or low self-esteem. People believe that someone else is more qualified or better situated to stand up and make a difference. But the truth is that most of the people who make a difference do so not because they are the best for the job but because they decided to try.

5. Make Tough Decisions and Stand by Them

When he was mayor of New York City, Rudy Giuliani kept a sign on his desk that stated, "I'm responsible." In his book *Leadership*, he wrote,

Throughout my career, I've maintained that accountability—the idea that the people who work for me are answerable to those we work for—is the cornerstone, and this starts with me . . . Nothing builds confidence in a leader more than the willingness to take responsibility for what happens during his watch. One might add that nothing builds a stronger case for holding employees to a high standard than a boss who holds himself to an even higher one. This is true in any organization, but it's particularly true in government.[8]

That mindset served him well during the crisis of 9/11 in 2001. He had to make many tough decisions very quickly. And whether they were right or wrong, he stood by them. His tough-minded responsibility coupled with strong leadership served the people well during that difficult time.

President Abraham Lincoln said, "You cannot escape the responsibility of tomorrow by evading it today." Easy decisions may make us look good, but making tough ones—and taking ownership of them—makes us better.

6. Live Beyond Yourself

There is one more aspect of responsibility that I want to share with you. It will take you beyond the level of those who simply take responsibility for themselves. It is the idea of taking responsibility beyond yourself by serving others. In a speech to the Massachusetts legislature on the eve of his presidency, John F. Kennedy said,

For of those to whom much is given, much is required. And when at some future date the high court of history sits in judgment on each one of us—recording whether in our brief

span of service we fulfilled our responsibilities to the state—
our success or failure, in whatever office we may hold, will
be measured by the answers to four questions. First, were we
truly men of courage[?] . . . Secondly, were we truly men of
judgement[?] . . . Third, were we truly men of integrity[?] . . .
Finally, were we truly men of dedication[?][9]

Self-serving people regard their talent and resources as what
they own. Serving people regard their talent and resources as
what's on loan.

Holocaust survivor Elie Wiesel, who won the Nobel Peace
Prize in 1986, spent the years after his time in the Nazi concentration camps trying to give back to others. He taught as
a professor at Boston University. He also traveled extensively
giving talks and sharing the wisdom he gained from his life
experiences. One of the questions he asked young people was,
"How will you cope with the privileges and obligations society
will feel entitled to place on you?" As he tried to guide them,
he shared his sense of responsibility to others:

What I receive I must pass on to others. The knowledge that
I have must not remain imprisoned in my brain. I owe it to
many men and women to do something with it. I feel the
need to pay back what was given to me. Call it gratitude . . .
To learn means to accept the postulate that life did not begin
at my birth. Others have been there before me, and I walk in
their footsteps.

Practicing responsibility will do great things for you. It will
strengthen your talent, advance your skills, and increase your
opportunities. It will improve your quality of life during the

day and help you sleep better at night. But it will also improve the lives of the people around you.

If you want your life to be a magnificent story, then realize you are its author. Every day you have the chance to write a new page in that story. I want to encourage you to fill those pages with responsibility to others and yourself. If you do, in the end you will not be disappointed.

CHAPTER 14

LEAN IN TO TEAMWORK

I n the Academy Award–winning movie *Rocky*, boxer Rocky Balboa describes his relationship with his girlfriend, Adrian: "I've got gaps. She's got gaps. But together we've got no gaps." What a wonderful description of teamwork! It doesn't matter how talented you may be—you have gaps. There are things you don't do well. What's the best way to handle your weaknesses? Partner with others who have strengths in those areas. If you want to do something *really* big, then do it as part of a team.

TEAMWORK TRUTHS

In 2001 when I wrote *The 17 Indisputable Laws of Teamwork*, the first law I included was the Law of Significance, which says, "One is too small a number to achieve greatness." If you want to do anything of value, teamwork is required.

Teamwork not only allows a person to do what he couldn't otherwise do; it also has a compounding effect on all he possesses—including talent. If you believe one person is a work of God (which I do), then a group of talented people committed to working together is a work of art. Whatever your vision or desire, teamwork makes the dream work.

Working together with other people toward a common goal is one of the most rewarding experiences of life. I've led or been part of many different kinds of teams—sports teams, work teams, business teams, ministry teams, communication teams, choirs, bands, committees, boards, you name it. I've observed teams of nearly every type in my travels around the world. And talking to leaders, developing teams, counseling with coaches, and teaching and writing on teamwork have influenced my thinking when it comes to teams. What I've learned I want to share with you:

1. TEAMWORK DIVIDES THE EFFORT AND MULTIPLIES THE EFFECT

Would you like to get better results from less work? I think everyone would. That's what teamwork provides. In his book *Jesus on Leadership*, C. Gene Wilkes describes why teamwork is superior to individual effort:

- Teams involve more people, thus affording more resources, ideas, and energy than an individual possesses.
- Teams maximize a leader's potential and minimize her weaknesses. Strengths and weaknesses are more exposed in individuals.
- Teams provide multiple perspectives on how to meet a need or reach a goal, thus devising several alternatives for each situation. Individual insight is seldom as broad and deep as a group's when it takes on a problem.

- Teams share the credit for victories and the blame for losses. This fosters genuine humility and authentic community. Individuals take credit and blame alone. This fosters pride and sometimes a sense of failure.
- Teams keep leaders accountable for the goal. Individuals connected to no one can change the goal without accountability.
- Teams can simply do more than an individual.[1]

It's common sense that people working together can do more than an individual working alone. So why are some people reluctant to engage in teamwork? It can be difficult in the beginning. Teams don't usually come together and develop on their own. They require leadership and cooperation. While that may be more work on the front end, the dividends it pays on the back end are tremendous and well worth the effort.

2. Talent Wins Games, but Teamwork Wins Championships

A sign in the New England Patriots' locker room states, "Individuals play the game, but teams win championships." Obviously the Patriot players understand this. They have won the Super Bowl six times.

Teams that repeatedly win championships are models of teamwork. For more than two decades, the Boston Celtics dominated the NBA. Their team has won more championships than any other in NBA history, and at one point during the fifties and sixties, the Celtics won eight championships in a row. During their run, the Celtics never had a player lead the league in scoring. Red Auerbach, who coached the Celtics and then later moved to their front office, always emphasized teamwork. He asserted, "One person seeking glory doesn't accomplish much; everything we've done has been the result of people working together to meet our common goals."

It's easy to see the fruit of teamwork in sports. But it is at least as important in business. Harold S. Geneen, who was director, president, and CEO of ITT for twenty years, observed, "The essence of leadership is the ability to inspire others to work together as a team—to stretch for a common objective." If you want to perform at the highest possible level, you need to be part of a team.

3. TEAMWORK IS NOT ABOUT YOU

The Harvard Business School recognizes a team as a small number of people with complementary skills who are committed to a common purpose, performance goals, and approach for which they hold themselves mutually accountable. Getting those people to work together is sometimes a challenge. It requires good leadership. And the more talented the team members, the better the leadership that is needed. The true measure of team leadership is not getting people to work. Neither is it getting people to work hard. The true measure of a leader is getting people to work hard together!

All great teams are the result of their players making decisions based on what's best for the rest. That's true in sports, business, the military, and volunteer organizations. And it's true at every level, from the part-time support person to the coach or CEO. The best leaders also put their team first. C. Gene Wilkes observes,

Team leaders genuinely believe that they do not have all the answers—so they do not insist on providing them. They believe they do *not* need to make all key decisions—so they do not do so. They believe they *cannot* succeed without the combined contributions of all the other members of the team to a common end—so they avoid any action that might constrain inputs or intimidate anyone on the team. Ego is *not* their predominant concern.[2]

Highly talented teams possess players with strong egos. One secret of successful teamwork is converting individual ego into team confidence, individual sacrifice, and synergy. Pat Riley, NBA champion coach, says, "Teamwork requires that everyone's efforts flow in a single direction. Feelings of significance happen when a team's energy takes on a life of its own."

4. Great Teams Create Community

All effective teams create an environment where relationships grow and teammates become connected to one another. To use a term that is currently popular, they create a *sense of community*. That environment of community is based on trust. Little can be accomplished without it.

On good teams, trust is a nonnegotiable. On winning teams, players extend trust to one another. Initially that is a risk because their trust can be violated and they can be hurt. At the same time that they are giving trust freely, they conduct themselves in such a way to earn trust from others. They hold themselves to a high standard. When everyone gives freely and bonds of trust develop and are tested over time, players begin to have faith in one another. They believe that the person next to them will act with consistency, keep commitments, maintain confidences, and support others. The stronger the sense of community becomes, the greater their potential to work together.

Developing a sense of community in a team does not mean there is no conflict. All teams experience disagreements. All relationships have tension. But you can work them out. When a team shares a strong sense of community, team members can resolve conflicts without dissolving relationships.

5. Adding Value to Others Adds Value to You

"My husband and I have a very happy marriage," a woman bragged. "There's nothing I wouldn't do for him, and there's nothing he wouldn't do for me. And that's the way we go through life—doing nothing for each other!" That kind of attitude is a certain road to disaster for any team—including a married couple.

Too often people join a team for their personal benefit. They want a supporting cast so that they can be the star. But that attitude hurts the team. When even the most talented person has a mind to serve, special things can happen. Former NBA great Magic Johnson paraphrased John F. Kennedy when he stated, "Ask not what your teammates can do for you. Ask what you can do for your teammates." That wasn't just talk for Johnson. Over the course of his career with the Los Angeles Lakers, he started in every position during championship games to help his team.

U.S. president Woodrow Wilson asserted, "You are not here merely to make a living. You are here in order to enable the world to live more amply, with greater vision, with a finer spirit of hope and achievement. You are here to enrich the world, and you impoverish yourself if you forget the errand."[3] People who take advantage of others inevitably fail in business and relationships. If you desire to succeed, then live by these four simple words: *add value to others*. That philosophy will take you far.

HOW TO LEAN IN TO TEAMWORK

All talented people have a choice to make: do their own thing and get all the credit, or do the team thing and share it. My observation is that not only do talented people accomplish more when working with others, but they are also more fulfilled than those who go it alone. My hope is that you choose teamwork over solo efforts. If that is your desire, then do the following:

1. Buy into the Law of Significance

Earlier in this chapter I mentioned the Law of Significance from *The 17 Indisputable Laws of Teamwork*: "One is too small a number to achieve greatness." In 2002, when I was teaching on the laws, I challenged members of the audience of ten thousand: "Name one person in the history of mankind who alone, without the help of anyone, made a significant impact on civilization."

A voice from the crowd yelled, "Charles Lindbergh—he crossed the Atlantic Ocean in a plane by himself."

The crowd cheered.

"That's true," I responded, and the crowd cheered louder, thinking I had been stumped. "But did you know," I continued, "that Ryan Aeronautical Engineering designed and built the plane? And did you know that ten millionaires financed the trip?" The crowd exploded. "Are there any more suggestions?" I asked.

I want to give you the same challenge. Think of any significant accomplishment that appears to be a solo act. Then do some research and you will find that others worked with the individuals or supported them so that they could do what they did. No one does anything significant on his own. One is too small a number to achieve greatness. If you buy into that idea, then you will embrace the concept of teamwork. And that will be the foundation upon which you multiply your talent and take it to the highest level.

2. Include a Team in Your Dream

Journalist and radio host Rex Murphy asserts, "The successful attainment of a dream is a cart and horse affair. Without a team of horses, a cart full of dreams can go nowhere." Teamwork gives you the best opportunity to turn your vision into reality. The greater the vision, the more need there is for a good team. But being willing to engage in teamwork is not the same as actively pursuing a team and becoming part of it. To succeed, you need to get on a team and find your best place in it. That may be as its leader, or it may not. Rudy Giuliani says,

> In reality, a leader *must* understand that success is best achieved through teamwork. From the moment you are put into a leadership position you must demonstrate ultimate humility. A leader must know his weaknesses in order to counterbalance them with the strengths of the team. When I became the Mayor of New York, I had both strengths and weaknesses. For instance, I did not have very much experience in economics. I found members for my team that had experience and great talent in the field of economics. When every member of the team is operating in his or her strengths, your organization will flourish. When crisis comes you will have the people in place to manage every situation with excellence.

If you're not certain about where you ultimately belong on a team, don't let that stop you from engaging in teamwork. Find others who are like-minded in their attitudes and passion, and join them.

3. DEVELOP YOUR TEAM

If you are a leader on your team, then you must make it your goal to develop your teammates or players. That process begins with having the right people on the team. It's said that people are known by the company they keep. But it can also be said that a company is known by the people it keeps. Jack Welch, former chairman and CEO of General Electric, observed, "If you pick the right people and give them the opportunity to spread their wings—and put compensation as a carrier behind it—you almost don't have to manage them." That's why Patrick Emington said, "It is the greatest folly to talk of motivating anybody. The real key is to help others to unlock and direct their deepest motivators."

The process continues with your doing whatever you can to help people grow and reach their potential. You must do your best to see the abilities of others and help them recognize and develop those abilities. That's what all good leaders do. They don't just become successful. They help others become successful.

4. GIVE THE CREDIT FOR SUCCESS TO THE TEAM

The final step to becoming a success in the area of teamwork is to give as much of the credit as you can to the people on the team. In his book *Good to Great*, Jim Collins points out that the leaders of the best organizations, what he calls "level-5 leaders," are characterized by humility and a tendency to avoid the spotlight.[4] Does that mean those leaders aren't talented? Of course not. Does it mean they have no egos? No. It means they recognize that everyone on the team is important, and they understand that people do better work and do it with greater effort when they are recognized for their contribution.

If you consider what top leaders and former CEOs have said about this, you'll recognize a pattern:

> "If I were to put someone on the front cover of *Business Week* or *Fortune*, it would be . . . the person who heads up our research organization, not me. Or I would put a team of people on the cover."[5]
>
> RAY GILMARTIN (MERCK)

> "I haven't done this [created the company's turnaround]. It's been 280,000 people who have done it. We took a change in focus, a change in preoccupation, and a great talented group of people . . . and changed the company."[6]
>
> LOU GERSTNER (IBM)

> "It's amazing what you can do when you don't seek all the credit. I find nothing is really one person's idea."[7]
>
> DAN TULLY (MERRILL LYNCH)

> "We have 68,000 employees. With a company this size, I'm not 'running the business' . . . My job is to create the environment that enables people to leverage each other beyond their own individual capabilities."[8]
>
> WALTER SHIPLEY (CITIBANK)

If you want to help your team go further and help team members sharpen their talent and maximize their potential, when things don't go well, take more than your fair share of the blame, and when things go well, give all of the credit away.

One person who captured my attention was Bono, singer for the rock band U2. I must admit, I was fairly late in discovering him. His music wasn't really my cup of tea. But his passion, leadership, and activism really impress me. In 2005, he was named a Person of the Year by *Time* magazine, along with Bill and Melinda Gates.

There's no doubting Bono's talent. His success in the musical world is obvious. He has penned many hit songs, and U2, which has been together for more than forty years, is one of the most successful bands in history. Together the band members have sold approximately 170 million albums.[9]

Bono has expanded his efforts beyond the world of music. He has become an advocate for African aid and economic development. And he's not just a celebrity lending his name to a cause. Senator Rick Santorum said of him, "Bono understands the issues better than 99% of the members of Congress."[10] And Bono has relentlessly worked at partnering with other people to further the causes he's passionate about. He has met with heads of state, economists, industry leaders, celebrities—anyone who has the potential to add value to the people he desires to help.

Where did Bono learn to rely on others, to be part of a team and enlist the aid of others? Rock stars are supposed to be self-absorbed, iconoclastic, isolated, and indifferent to others. That is what happens to many famous people, and it's the reason many music groups don't stay together. Bono comments,

There's moments when people are so lost in their own selves, the demands of their own life, that it's very hard to be in a band . . . People want to be lords of their own domain. I mean, everybody, as they get older . . . rids the room of argument. You see it in your family, you see it with your friends, and they get a smaller and smaller circle of people around them, who agree with them. And life ends up with a dull sweetness.[11]

What is Bono's secret, after having been a rock star for more than twenty-five years? He learned teamwork in the band. Bono recognizes his need for others and, in fact, says he can't imagine having been a solo artist. He admits,

The thing that'll make you less and less able to realize your potential is a room that's empty of argument. And I would be terrified to be on my own as a solo singer, not to have a band to argue with. I mean, I surround myself with argument, and a band, a family of very spunky kids, and a wife who's smarter than anyone. I've got a lot of very smart friends, a whole extended family of them . . . You're as good as the arguments you get. So maybe the reason why the band hasn't split up is that people might get this: that even though they're only one quarter of U2, they're more than they would be if they were one whole of something else. I certainly feel that way.[12]

I can't think of a better way to say it myself. A talented person who is part of a team—in the right place on the right team—becomes more than he ever could on his own. That's what it means to be a success.

Notes

Chapter 1: Commit to Choices that Bring Success

1. Peter Drucker, *The Effective Executive* (New York: HarperCollins, 2006), 1.

2. Robert J. Kriegel and Louis Patler, *If It Ain't Broke . . . Break It!* (New York: Warner Books, 1991), 11.

3. Dr. Seuss, *Oh, The Places You'll Go* (New York: Random House, 1990).

Chapter 2: Believe in Yourself

1. Joel Garfinkle, *Dream Job Coaching* (2004–2005). http://www.dreamjobcoaching.com/articles/court -martial.html. Used with permission. All rights reserved.

2. Robert J. Kriegel and Louis Patler, *If It Ain't Broke . . . Break It*! (New York: Warner Books, 1992), 44.

3. Sharon Wood, *Rising: Becoming the First North American Woman on Everest* (Seattle, WA: Mountaineers Books, 2019).

4. Martin Seligman, *Learned Optimism: How to Change Your Mind and Your Life* (New York: Pocket Books, 1998), 99.

5. From Walter D. Wintle, "The Man Who Thinks He Can,"

Poems That Live Forever, comp. Hazel Felleman (New York: Doubleday, 1965), 310.

6. Neil Simon, "Commencement address Williams College, MA" (22 June 1984), https://www.csmonitor.com/1984 /0622/062200.html.

7. Christopher Reeve, "1996 Democratic National Convention," (convention address, Chicago, IL, 26 August 1996), https:// www.americanrhetoric.com/speeches/christopherreeve1996dnc .htm.

8. Harvey Mackay, *The Mackay MBA of Selling in the Real World* (New York: Penguin, 2011), 30.

9. Robert H. Schuller, *Tough Times Never Last, but Tough People Do!* (New York: Bantam, 1984), 204, emphasis added.

Chapter 3: Fire Up Your Passion

1. Robert J. Kriegel and Louis Patler, *If It Ain't Broke . . . Break It!* (New York: Warner Books, 1992), 259.

2. Martin Luther King, Jr., "Address at the Freedom Rally in Cobo Hall" (speech, Detroit, MI, 23 June 1963), https://kinginstitute.stanford.edu /king-papers/documents/address-freedom-rally-cobo-hall.

3. Richard Edler, *If I Knew Then What I Know Now: CEOs and Other Smart Executives Share Wisdom They Wish They'd Been Told 25 Years Ago* (New York: Berkley 1995), 185.

4. Daniel Ruettiger, "Rise Above with Rudy," *Rudy International*, https://www.rudyinternational.com.

Chapter 4: Initiate Action

1. Les Brown, *You've Got to Be HUNGRY: The GREATNESS Within to Win* (Miami, FL: Brown Family Publishing, 2020).

2. Katherine Paterson, *Jacob Have I Loved* (New York: HarperCollins, 1980), 58.

3. Proverbs 6:6–11, *The Message: The New Testament in Contemporary English*, by Eugene H. Peterson. Copyright © 1993, 1994, 1995, 1996, 2000.

4. Robert A. Mamis, "How to Manage Your Sales Force: A Successful Manager Gives Tips on Creating a Winning Sales Team," *Inc.com* (1 January 1990), https://www.inc.com/magazine/19900101/5011.html.

5. John Maxwell, *The 21 Irrefutable Laws of Leadership: Follow Them and People Will Follow You* (Nashville, TN: Thomas Nelson, 1998, 2007).

6. Edgar A. Guest, "To-morrow," *A Heap O' Livin'* (Chicago: Reilly and Lee, 1916).

7. Maxwell, *The 21 Irrefutable Laws of Leadership*.

Chapter 5: Focus Your Energy

1. Williams Matthews, *Getting on in the World: Or, Hints on Success in Life* (London: Ward, Lock, & Tyler, Warwick House, 1874), 77.

2. Richard E. Byrd, *Alone: The Classic Story of His Greatest Adventure* (Washington, DC: Island Press, 1938), 189.

3. Donald E. Demaray, *Laughter, Joy, and Healing* (Grand Rapids: Baker Book House, 1986), 34–35.

4. Lewis Carroll, *Through the Looking Glass* (New York: Macmillan, 1871, 2009), 64.

5. Elbert Hubbard, *A Message to Garcia: And Other Essential Writings on Success* (1899).

6. Peter Drucker, *Managing for Results* (New York: HarperCollins, 1993), 11.

7. Anthony Campolo, speech made in Indianapolis, quoted in Zig Ziglar, *Raising Positive Kids in a Negative World* (New York: Ballantine Books, 1996), 98–99.

Chapter 6: Value Preparation

1. Don Beveridge Jr. and Jeffrey P. Davidson, *The Achievement Challenge: How to Be a 10 in Business* (Homewood, IL: Irwin Professional, 1987).

2. The New American Standard Bible®, Copyright © The Lockman Foundation 1960, 1962, 1963, 1968, 1971, 1972, 1973, 1975, 1977. Used by permission. (www.Lockman.org).

3. Kathleen M. Eisenhardt, "Making Fast Strategic Decisions in High-Velocity Environments," *Academy of Management Journal*, Vol. 32, No. 3 (Sept. 1989), 543–76.

Chapter 7: Embrace Practice

1. *Reader's Digest* (New York: January 1992), 91.

2. Jon Johnston, *Christian Excellence* (Grand Rapids: Baker Book House, 1985), 30.

Chapter 8: Embody Perseverance

1. Adapted from Max Isaacson, *How to Conquer the Fear of Public Speaking and Other Coronary Threats* (Rockville Centre, NY: Farnsworth Publishing, 1984), 77.

2. Howard Goodman, "I Don't Regret a Mile," used by permission. Rick Goodman, Goodman and Associates, P.O. Box 158778, Nashville, TN 37215.

3. "One List," *Houston Chronicle* (1 January 2001).

4. Pat Riley, *The Winner Within* (New York: Penguin, 1993), 263.

5. George E. Vaillant, *Aging Well: Surprising Guideposts to a Happier Life from the Landmark Harvard Study of Adult Development* (New York: Little, Brown and Company, 2003), 285.

6. Bruce Nash, *The Football Hall of Shame* (New York: Pocket Books, 1991), 21–22.

Chapter 9: Demonstrate Courage

1. C. S. Lewis, *The Screwtape Letters* (New York: HarperOne, 2001), 161.

2. Ralph Waldo Emerson, *The Complete Works of Ralph Waldo Emerson: Society and Solitude* (1904).

3. John C. Maxwell, *Winning with People: Discover the People Principles That Work for You Every Time* (Nashville: Thomas Nelson, 2004), 221.

4. C.V. White, quoted in *Chicago the Great Central Market: A Magazine of Business* (January, 1907), 76.

5. Pat Williams, *American Scandal: The Solution for the Crisis of Character* (Shippensburgh, PA: Treasure House, 2003), 290.

6. Thomas Edison, address given in New Jersey (1931).

Chapter 10: Become More Teachable

1. Philip B. Crosby, *Quality Is Free* (New York: Penguin, 1980), 68.

2. Konrad Hölé, *Diamonds for Daily Living* (World Press, 1996).

3. Dave Anderson, "The Number One Cause of Management Failure," *Social Media Today* (27 April 2008), https://www.socialmediatoday.com/content/guest-article-number-one-cause-management-failure-dave-anderson.

4. Proverbs 26:12, New King James Version®. Copyright © 1982 by Thomas Nelson, Inc. Used by permission. All rights reserved.

5. C. S. Lewis, *The C.S. Lewis Signature Classics* (New York: HarperOne, 2017), 108.

6. Michael E. Angier, *101 Best Ways to Get Ahead: Solid Gold Advice from 101 of the World's Most Successful People* (South Burlington, Vermont: Success Networks International, Inc., 2005), 60.

7. Eric W. Johnson, ed., *A Treasury of Humor* (New York: Ivy Books, 1990), 304.

Chapter 11 Develop Strong Character

1. Pat Williams, *Coach Wooden: The 7 Principles That Shaped His Life and Will Change Yours* (Grand Rapids, MI: Baker), 41–42.

2. Pat Williams, *American Scandal: The Solution for the Crisis of Character* (Shippensburg, PA: Treasure House, 2003), 105.

3. August C. Bolino, *Men of Massachusetts: Bay State Contributors to American Society* (Bloomington, IL: iUniverse, 2012), 386.

4. Stan Mooneyham, *Dancing on the Strait and Narrow* (San Francisco: Harper and Row, 1989), 1–2, 68.

5. Craig Lambert, "Bobby Jones: Brief life of a golf legend: 1902–1971," *Harvard Magazine* (March–April 2002), https://www.harvardmagazine.com/2002/03/bobby-jones.html.

6. Stephen Covey, *The Seven Habits of Highly Effective People: Restoring the Character Ethic* (New York: Simon and Schuster, 1989), 21.

7. Martin Luther King, Jr., "A Proper Sense of Priorities speech," delivered February 6, 1968, in Washington, DC. http://www.aavw.org/special_features/speeches_speech_king04.html.

Chapter 12: Cultivate Good Relationships

1. John Wooden, *My Personal Best: Life Lessons from an All-American Journey* (New York: McGraw-Hill, 2004).

2. Les Parrott, *High-Maintenance Relationships* (Wheaton, IL: Tyndale, 1997).

3. Helen Keller, *The Story of My Life* (New York: Doubleday, 1905), 140.

4. Ralph Waldo Emerson, "Glory of Friendship," in *Emerson's Essays on Manners, Self-Reliance, Compensation, Nature, Friendship* (Chicago, IL: Longmans, Green, and Co., 1915).

5. Lee Iacocca, *Iacocca: An Autobiography* (New York: Bantam, 1984), 60.

6. Emerson, *Emerson's Essays*.

7. Gay Zenola MacLaren, *Morally We Roll Along* (Boston: Brown and Co., 1938), 66.

8. William Arthur Ward, *Fountains of Faith: The Words of William Arthur Ward* (Anderson, SC: Droke House, 1970).

Chapter 13: Commit to Responsibility

1. Michael Korda, *Success! How Every Man and Woman Can Achieve It* (New York: Random House, 1977), 14.

2. Tony Campolo, *The Covenant Companion*, April 1998.

3. Gillian Flynn, "Pinnacle Brands: A Strike Puts Employees Up to Bat," *Personnel Journal,* Vol. 75, No. 6 (June 1996), 71–74, https://www.workforce.com/news/pinnacle-brands-a-strike-puts-employees-up-to-bat.

4. Richard L. Evans, *The Improvement Era* (Provo, UT: General Board of the Mutual Improvement Associations, 1965), 704.

5. Pat Williams, *American Scandal: The Solution for the Crisis of Character* (Shippensburgh, PA: Treasure House, 2003), 174–75.

6. Elaine J. Hom, "Oprah Winfrey Biography," *Business News Daily* (24 January 2019), https://www.businessnewsdaily.com/4080-business-profile-oprah-winfrey.html.

7. Ron French, "Forget Responsibility, Blame Someone Else," found in "Bestowing Blame" by Dr. David H. McKinley, *Good Bad Habits* (19 February 2003), https://docplayer.net/137434979-Powerlunch-honesty-is-the-best-policy-dr-david-h-mckinley-l-i-f-e-n-o-t-e-s-w-e-d-n-e-s-d-a-y-j-a-n-u-a-r-y-1–5.html.

8. Rudolph W. Giuliani with Ken Kurson, *Leadership* (New York: Hyperion, 2002), 69–70.

9. John F. Kennedy speech to Massachusetts legislature (9 January 1961), quoted on www.mass.gov/statehouse/jfk _speech.htm.

Chapter 14: Lean In to Teamwork

1. C. Gene Wilkes, *Jesus on Leadership: Timeless Wisdom on Servant Leadership* (Carol Stream, IL: Tyndale, 1998), 212

2. Ibid., 224.

3. President Woodrow Wilson, address given at Swarthmore College, Swarthmore, PA, (October 25, 1913), https://archive.org /stream/addressofpreside07wilsonw/addressofpreside07wilsonw _djvu.txt.

4. Jim Collins, *Good to Great: Why Some Companies Make the Leap and Others Don't* (New York: HarperCollins, 2001), 5, 22.

5. Thomas J. Neff and James M. Citrin, *Lessons from the Top* (New York: Currency/Doubleday, 2001), 149.

6. Ibid., 140.

7. Ibid., 312.

8. Ibid., 273.

9. Udo Merkel, *Power, Politics and International Events: Socio-cultural Analyses of Festivals and Spectacles* (New York: Routledge, 2014), 174–190.

10. Josh Tyrangiel, "The Constant Charmer," *Time*, 26 December–2 January 2006, 50.

11. Michka Assayas, *Bono in Conversation with Michka Assayas* (New York: Riverhead Books, 2005), 151.

12. Ibid., 152.

About the Author

John C. Maxwell is a #1 *New York Times* bestselling author, coach, and speaker who has sold more than thirty-one million books in fifty languages. He has been identified as the #1 leader in business by the American Management Association® and the most influential leadership expert in the world by *Business Insider* and *Inc.* magazine. He is the founder of the John Maxwell Company, the John Maxwell Team, EQUIP, and the John Maxwell Leadership Foundation, organizations that have trained millions of leaders from every country of the world. A recipient of the Horatio Alger Award, as well as the Mother Teresa Prize for Global Peace and Leadership from the Luminary Leadership Network, Dr. Maxwell speaks each year to *Fortune* 500 companies, presidents of nations, and many of the world's top business leaders. He can be followed at Twitter.com/JohnCMaxwell. For more information about him visit JohnMaxwell.com.